Who's Teaching Who?

by Thornton Cline

Vertū Publishing, 2022
A Component of Vertū Marketing, LLC

Copyright © 2022 by Vertū Publishing

All rights reserved. No part of this publication may be reproduced, distributed, or transmitted in any form or by any means, including photocopying, recording, or other electronic or mechanical methods, without the prior written permission of the publisher, except in the case of brief quotations embodied in critical reviews and certain other noncommercial uses permitted by copyright law. For permission requests, write to the publisher, addressed "Attention: Permissions Coordinator," at the enail address below.

VERTŪ PUBLISHING

A Component of Vertū Marketing LLC

www.vertumarketing.com

Ordering Information:

Quantity sales. Special discounts are available on quantity purchases by corporations, associations, and others. For details, contact the publisher at the address above.

Orders by U.S. trade bookstores and wholesalers.

Please contact: Tel: (866) 779-0795.

publishing@vertu-marketing.com

Printed in the United States of America

ISBN 979-8-9855404-8-2

To all of my students.

CONTENTS

Chapter One
Why I Wrote This Book 1
Chapter Two
Corey: Patience 6
Chapter Three
Mia: Joy 21
Chapter Four
Zane: Empathy 29
Chapter Five
Daniel: Perseverance 38
Chapter Six
Lizzy: Compassion 45
Chapter Seven
Louis: Forgiveness 52
Chapter Eight
Jeff: Love 60
Chapter Nine
Roxie: Passion 71
Chapter Ten
Elijah: Motivation 76
Chapter Eleven
Tina: Hard work 83
Chapter Twelve
Gabby: Compassion 89
Chapter Thirteen
Jeremy: Determination 96
Chapter Fourteen
Amber: Courage 102
Chapter Fifteen
Seth: Creativity 108
Chapter Sixteen
 Leah: Humor 115
Chapter Seventeen
Stuart: Persistence 121
Chapter Eighteen
The Conclusion 127
Acknowledgements 132
About the Author 133

CHAPTER ONE:

WHY I WROTE THIS BOOK

When you look at me now, you don't see the me I used to be. I'm a different person who evolved through the influence of the music students I've taught. Everyone has been either a student or teacher in some capacity, whether in a traditional classroom, homeschooling setting, or job training. This book you are about to read is an affirmation of the students I have instructed for more than four decades, and I hope it will inspire and motivate you in your teaching moments and in life in general.

This book is *not* a memoir or a biography. These stories are not about which students I favored or didn't or which students were the best in my eyes. All of my students made a positive difference in my life. Every one of them enriched my life in some way, whether it be insignificant or major. I hope that, somehow, I have enriched their lives too.

I couldn't write a book about all my students because it would be a massive tome. I have had the opportunity to teach over six thousand students (yes, you read that right) in private, public, and group situations (choir, orchestra, and Suzuki groups) from age two up to grandparents in their seventies and eighties. I have taught students in eight different states in the United States.

Teaching is one of my passions, and I love the interaction of the student with the teacher. Some of my pupils have been with me for decades. They are family to me. I have experienced victories and hardships with my students and their families. I have attended many ceremonies through my association with all the families—weddings, graduations, concerts, recitals, and some confirmations and baptisms. I have played my violin, piano, and cello for many of my students' weddings. I felt honored that they asked.

Many of my students have received scholarships to universities all over the world, totaling millions of dollars in scholarship monies. Some of my students have become professional musicians who are playing in major orchestras or have signed to major record labels and have gained recognition around the world for their musical achievements. Some have performed for dignitaries such as kings and queens. I am currently in my second generation of students. The students I taught have grown up and had children who are now studying music with me. These parents of second-generation students often tell fond stories of how Mr. Cline taught them a certain way and about how funny Mr. Cline was in the lessons. It is so refreshing to see how the second-generation students react to their moms or dads who share happy memories of their studies with me. It is also interesting to see how their children respond to me compared to their parents when they studied music lessons.

I continue to teach and suspect I will be teaching until I take my last breath. Why would teachers want to stop instructing if they are enjoying it, it makes them happy, and they are capable of teaching? Teaching is a mission for me, and I have found my purpose in life while on this earth. Some of my students' parents have complimented me over the years by praising my teaching. Many have remarked that I am a gifted and talented teacher. Education has always been second nature to me and has come easy. So, in a sense, you could call my teaching a gift. While I have continued to take additional workshop training and have always updated my skills, teaching has never been difficult for me. I continuously pour my heart and soul into every one of my students. I teach them as if they were my children.

Sometimes I run into some of my students in the grocery store or at a public event. I hear from past students from time to time on Facebook, through email, or with a card sent to me through the US Mail. Admittedly, I can't remember the names of all my students. But just because I can't remember every one of their names doesn't minimize any one of them. I still have learned something from all of them. But there are some of my students whom I cannot forget.

I would love to hear from the readers of this book. If you feel like you've learned something from one or some of these students, please send me an email at ThorntonClineauthor@gmail.com. I would love to hear the stories from your lives.

CHAPTER TWO:

COREY

(PATIENCE)

When Corey's grandparents signed him up for private piano lessons with me (his parents weren't interested in having him study music), Corey was in the fourth grade and hungered for music; it was in his blood and genes. I later learned that some of his cousins, aunts, and uncles were professional musicians, and one became famous in the early days of country music. Corey's family was mighty proud of their famed relative and made it known to everyone who that famous singer was and what he had accomplished. Since I am in the music business, including writing songs, I could relate to the pride of a family and student who had a famous country music singer.

On the surface, Corey was a happy-go-lucky kind of kid. He didn't seem to worry about life, his past, or the future, but once you got to know him and he revealed more of his personal life, Corey showed his true self. Corey was a charming boy with freckles, dimples, and a mischievous smile. The way he always dressed was "cool" with the latest fashion jeans and shirts, and his short, wavy, dirty-blonde hair still had that sophisticated look. The other students always commented on how fashionable and cool Corey dressed. His manner of dress so influenced some that they tried to copy him. It was funny to see how Corey's admirers would begin to get the "Corey look." Their admiration for Corey's style made him smile and feel confident at times.

Corey could talk all day long if you had the time to listen. He rambled about anything that came into his head. Everything seemed to interest him. He told what he thought were some pretty funny jokes and expected you to laugh even when they weren't really funny. I remember one time when I was in the middle of teaching Corey a song on the piano, he suddenly interrupted the lesson.

"Hey, Mr. Cline, did you hear the one about the clown and the teacher?" Corey asked.

"No, Corey, I didn't," I replied. "We need to get back to playing the piano."

Corey folded his arms in protest as if I had offended him.

"But don't you want to hear my joke?" he asked, leaning his body toward me and raising his head in eager expectation.

"Yes, but not now," I answered. "I'll listen to your joke after our piano lesson."

I stood my ground with Corey and folded my own arms as if to say, "No more playing around. We need to get down to business." Corey was good at manipulation and could make someone feel guilty for not going along with his idea. But I continued to stand firm, insisting on no jokes or interruptions until after the lesson was over. Corey finally backed down and returned his focus to the piece he was learning.

Corey had a natural ability to play the piano. Because he had such a great ear, he could play almost any song, from beginning level to advanced, without ever reading the music. This gift showed itself early at our very first lesson. When I started teaching Corey, he had never studied the piano before. I was quite amazed at his natural talent and was excited about developing his potential from the first day I taught him. Corey would proudly show off his gift to me by playing a new pop song he had taught himself. I would always react with enthusiasm and show great excitement for his gift. He appreciated any praise I offered.

From time to time, Corey showed his pride and confidence in his ability to learn advanced piano pieces.

"Look at this, Mr. Cline," Corey exclaimed.

Then he would show me how well he could play Beethoven's "Fur Elise" by memory.

"That is awesome, Corey," I replied with sincere praise.

Corey would smile and hold his shoulders and head up high whenever I offered a positive reaction or compliment.

I was amazed at how much Corey could achieve on the piano with his severe attention deficit disorder. His diagnosis was never kept in check because his parents and grandparents were either in denial or didn't think ADD was an important issue to address. His teachers held a different opinion on his disability. Corey was disruptive in school and often received demerits or detention for his unruly behavior in class. Before attending the school where I taught him the piano, Corey had hopped among several schools. Our student-teacher relationship clicked from the beginning, and he functioned well one-on-one in a private teaching scenario. Corey and I did some kind of bonding, perhaps because I took an interest in his talent and worked hard with him to encourage him to excel in his music.

Corey would surprise me sometimes with a kind word or two, complimenting me.

"You know, Mr. Cline, you are an awesome teacher," Corey confessed. "I like you."

"That's kind of you to say, Corey," I replied. "I like you too."

Finally, Corey's parents gave in to the faculty pressure that Corey should see a doctor to get diagnosed and hopefully receive some treatment for his ADD. So, his parents took Corey to a doctor, and he received a formal diagnosis. His doctor prescribed either Adderall or Ritalin to help Corey focus in class and keep his disruptive behavior in check. The medicine seemed to do the trick; however, I remember

Corey objecting to the medication and complaining about how it made him feel.

I vividly remember one piano lesson when Cory said, "Mr. Cline, I'm having a heart attack. My chest is hurting, and my heart is racing super-fast."

I realized that the drug was probably making Corey feel uncomfortable, and he was not used to it yet. "Oh, dear. Do I need to send you to the nurse's office?" I asked.

Corey knew I had his number, and he knew I had busted him for being so overdramatic. But he continued to complain. I stopped my teaching and walked over to the phone and picked up the mouthpiece.

"I'll call the nurse's office, and she can take care of you right now," I said.

Corey immediately jumped off the piano bench and dramatically waved his hands to indicate my call wouldn't be necessary.

"Mr. Cline, I'm okay. My heart will be okay," Corey replied.

"You sure you don't need to go down to the nurse's office and get checked out?" I asked.

"No, I'll be fine," Corey answered.

After that dramatic scene, Cory quieted down, and I never heard another mention of his chest pains from a heart attack or about his heart racing too fast. I knew at the time that Corey was seeking attention and crying out for help. But he needed a different kind of support, not medical care. When I reacted with my offer to help Corey medically, he knew his drama wasn't paying off like he thought it would. So, Corey returned to his quiet, subdued self under the influence of the ADD medication. Corey never spoke of his medical problems from that day forward and was somewhat subdued and mellow during all of his future lessons. I could tell Corey didn't like the quiet side of himself under the influence of ADD medicine. He was used to his bubbly, jovial, and hyper side. This fun-loving part of him was the side of Corey he liked the most about himself, and it seemed to hurt him that all of the teachers saw this as disruptive behavior. It was as if Corey lost all of his creativity and personality when he began taking his medicine.

Corey continued music lessons through the first year, as he was performing level four and five classical piano songs with ease. Despite being just a beginner himself, Corey could play circles around any other first-level student. I could tell his performances made him happy and built up his confidence, which he badly needed. Still, something was missing. Corey was not his true self and many times appeared to be in an almost zombie or unconscious state.

When I tell you the story of Corey's family life, I am not saying it with any judgment or condemnation. I am sharing the facts as they were in Corey's life. Corey had a rough family life up until age eleven. Because his parents were divorced, he was shuffled back and forth between his mother and his dad, and his grandparents also shared some custodial responsibilities. Corey had a brief stay in a foster home, but his mom convinced the court to let Corey return to her custody. His mother, with live-in boyfriends, worked all night as a stripper and a pole dancer for a gentleman's club in the downtown area. Many times, she arrived home at six a.m. just before Corey had to leave for school.

Corey's mom would end up taking Corey to school scantily dressed in her attire from her work at the club and usually high on cocaine to keep her awake during her overnight shift. Corey's dad, with come-and-go girlfriends, sold drugs on the streets downtown. He would usually party all night with alcohol and drugs.

Corey's dad usually slept all day, so he wasn't much involved in Corey's life. He was in and out of jail through most of Corey's childhood. When Corey was eight years old, his dad used him to sell drugs on the streets. Corey confessed to me that his dad had put him up to begging strangers for money or enticing them into drug deals with his dad. His dad was a master manipulator and con artist. He had a way with words, and he was charming and persuasive. What's worse is Corey's dad taught Corey how to be manipulative, charming, and persuasive. Corey was always resentful of how his dad treated him. He had no positive role models and never received compliments or praise from his parents. In fact, they were so against Corey studying piano and guitar with me that during a court battle between his two parents, Corey's mom threatened to steal Corey's guitar and sell it in revenge for his dad not paying her child support and alimony. I felt helpless and sickened when I heard these things, and I often prayed for Corey and his parents for some resolution to their continued bickering and court battles. In my opinion, no kid should ever have to experience that kind of treatment, especially from his or her parents.

But this isn't a perfect world, and sometimes life isn't fair. I believe I was supposed to meet Corey and to teach him. Perhaps I was the counterbalance to his awful, unstable life. Maybe I was the sunshine that brought Corey joy when all he was getting at home was thunder, lightning, and heavy storms. Whatever the case may be, I hope I helped Corey in some way and helped to influence his life positively.

Corey often complained about how, when he collected money begging on the streets, he had to surrender all of the money to his dad.

"It's not fair how my dad gets to keep all the money I helped him make," Corey protested. I could tell he resented his father. Worst of all, he felt used and worthless.

Corey breathed heavily and folded his arms as he shared his frustration. His face turned a deep red like an overripe watermelon. I responded with soft, kind, and gentle words.

"I'm sorry, Corey. Life isn't always fair," I replied.

Corey raised his voice to a fever pitch and shouted in anger. I could see he was venting, and I allowed Corey to release all of his rage and frustration. "My dad uses it for his beer and pot," Corey disclosed.

Again, I replied with gentle words. "I'm sorry," I said, trying not to sound judgmental.

I learned other information from Corey, whether true or not. He would tell me wild stories of the violent fights his dad got into and how once his dad killed a man by slitting his throat. He swore his dad never got caught for the crime because his dad disposed of the body in some wooded area. Sometimes, kids can either exaggerate or distort the truth. So, I took what Corey told me with a skeptical view. I did report the incidents of Corey being used to sell drugs on the street and the story of his dad supposedly killing a man and never getting caught for the crime. The principal looked at me as though I were gullible and falling for another of Corey's tall tales. Still, I felt it was my civic duty to report any possible crimes. Nothing ever happened as a result of my reporting what Corey told me. So, either Corey was exaggerating about his dad to get attention, or perhaps the principal didn't take the charges seriously. Or the principal did report Corey's information, but the police never found any evidence of Corey's dad having committed any crimes.

One day, Corey's mom showed up at the school's office. It was the middle of February, and she was wearing a halter top and a revealing micro mini skirt without a coat. Her arms and legs were covered in tattoos. Her clothes and body reeked of alcohol, cigarettes, cheap perfume, marijuana, and sex. Because it was a school day, parents, teachers, and students were coming in and out of the office, and the veteran principal of almost fifty years nearly had a coronary when she saw Corey's mom dressed the way she was. She tried to remain composed and professional, but it was impossible to miss how the odors from the woman's body filled the room. The principal gave Corey's mom a long winter coat to drape over her exposed body.

I remembered the story of Mary Magdalene with Jesus in the Bible. I know we must be careful not to judge another person as we are all sinners and have fallen short of God's glory. We don't know someone's life and what they've been through until we have lived inside their soul, mind, heart, and body. Who knows if a lot of what I heard about Corey's family was merely gossip instead of truth. I taught in a small town, and sometimes people in close-knit communities tend to gossip a lot. Sometimes it is hard to separate fact from fiction. I was professional and careful not ever to repeat any of these stories to anyone. They remained inside my brain and heart until today as I am writing this story. You can see why I decided not to use anyone's real name in this book.

Corey continued to study the piano with me and make extraordinary progress until the fifth grade. It was then that Corey's grandmother decided she wanted him to study private guitar lessons and continue with the piano. In my enthusiasm and naivety, I thought it would be a good idea for him to study both instruments as it would develop Corey's musical skills and make him a "complete" musician. My mentor in graduate school in New York had always emphasized teaching and learning more than one instrument for just that reason. The private dual music instrument study would have probably been an excellent idea for other students, but it was not for Corey.

Corey's grandmother signed him up for both private acoustic guitar lessons and piano lessons, which meant he would be pulled out of his academic classes at least twice a week. Corey was already struggling with his academic work, and he needed every minute of his classwork to succeed in school. I soon started receiving much flak from the teachers and administration. They believed Corey's music lessons were detrimental to his academic studies. In so many words, they blamed me for his declining grades and lack of educational interest. They strongly suggested that Corey quit his piano and guitar or at least his extra lessons in guitar. Most of the time, the faculty was very supportive of teaching private music lessons at the school. The faculty always spoke highly of my teaching and praised my work by saying how much the music lessons had helped the students to perform with higher test scores and to make good grades. But with Corey, the faculty was not behind me, and sometimes they snubbed me for continuing to teach Corey when they had advised against it.

Meanwhile, as Corey's grades went down, he was sent to detention almost every day. His family life became much tougher than before. Corey's mom and dad were openly fighting and playing childish, spiteful games of revenge. They were battling in court over who would have custody of Corey. Every day at school, Corey would report to me and his teachers about how the court deliberations were going and openly worried about what his fate would be. He would present both sides to the teachers. Corey talked about what it would be like to live with his mother and then present the case for living with his father. Corey couldn't stand either one of them, and their battles resulted in Corey's troubled life. While the court deliberated over which parent was fit enough to raise Corey, Corey's dad got locked up for selling drugs to a minor downtown, and it looked like his dad would spend a long time in jail. The court ruled in favor of Corey's mother to allow her custody of Corey.

This topsy-turvy, backward-and-forward uncertainty created havoc on Corey's life. He was like a boat tossed to and fro by the waves, lost in the deep seas. Not only was Corey failing every academic class at school except his music class with me, but his behavior was also unruly. Corey had violent mood swings where he could be quiet and peaceful one minute, and the next minute he could blow up like a bomb. All his woes culminated until he exploded one day with boiling rage. That was the final straw for the faculty and administration.

One day in PE, all hell broke loose. The coach asked Corey to do push-ups as part of the student's daily routine requirement. Corey openly refused to obey the coach's instructions. Coach gave him a demerit, and Corey's pent-up anger erupted out of nowhere. His face turned a deep red, and he started wildly swinging his fists at the coach. He punched the coach several times and then went on a rampage of swinging his fists at the other students. Corey knocked one student to the floor and gave another student a black eye and a concussion. He shouted and screamed obscenities at the coach and the students. Finally, the coach was able to apprehend Corey and pin him down while the principal intervened.

The school called his mom to take her son home. At first, she grumbled and complained that she was sleeping and couldn't be bothered with things that were the school's fault. After the school threatened to call child services and the juvenile court, Corey's mom got dressed and took her sweet time getting to the school. When she arrived, she lashed out at the principal with loud, piercing obscenities and shook her fists threateningly when the principal threatened to call the sheriff if she didn't back off. That was a scene every faculty, principal, or administration dreads facing. It was a nightmare from hell, and I give the principal and school credit for handling the situation calmly and professionally.

Corey's mother threatened to badmouth the school to the Better Business Bureau and smear the school's reputation. As she dragged Corey from the building, his mother shouted that she would take her son to a much better school. That was the last I saw of him. The school indefinitely suspended Corey. As often as I tried to reach out and inquire about Corey to his grandparents and his mother, I was unable to reach them. No one ever returned my emails, texts, and phone calls. I am not sure whether Corey's parents and grandmother were angry at me or just didn't want to have anything to do with me because I was associated with that "terrible school." I was greatly bothered by Corey's permanent suspension and about how the students and the coach were affected. Frustrated by my lack of ability to reach or help Corey, I turned to prayer for Corey and his entire family.

My hope and prayers are that I positively influenced Corey during those difficult times in his childhood. I hope and pray he will turn out well even though he has everything going against him. I also pray that God will bring peace to Corey's parents. Maybe in time, their wounds will heal and they will stop blaming the school and the teachers for all of Corey's problems. I sincerely believe that the faculty and administration did all they could to help Corey try to succeed. I know I gave him more than just excellent instruction on piano and guitar. I tried to be a great teacher and mentor to Corey. Perhaps, somewhere down the road, my attempts to shape his natural musical abilities will positively change him as he moves from his adolescent ages through his adult years. I don't know if that is reality or wishful thinking. But my dream is to meet Corey again one day and see him as a positively changed adult.

I do know for sure how much Corey changed my life through the short time I knew him. I've heard it said that when we teach others, we learn a great deal about ourselves. I always swore I would never be a judgmental person in life. But as hard as I tried not to judge, I failed miserably at trying not to form a "first impression" of someone I had just met or to have my teaching or thinking clouded with a bias of any kind. After getting to know Corey and his family, I began to find it easier to withhold my judgments of others and to become a person who doesn't form opinions about others based on externals. And although I didn't instantly change, but I gradually realized that if I judge others, they might judge me. And since I am nowhere near being perfect as a human being or teacher, I prefer to leave the judging to God, who is holy and perfect.

Corey also showed me how to have more empathy, patience, and compassion for another human being. Corey didn't choose his parents or his grandparents. Because Corey was only eleven years old, he had no choice as to where he would live or where he would grow up. Either his parents, his grandparents, or the courts made those decisions for him. And until he became an adult, he would have to abide by his parents, grandparents, or the court's wishes for his welfare. I am sure I had a small influence in Corey's life, but I was helpless and powerless to make any significant decisions for Corey.

I am grateful for being a part of Corey's life and for Corey's coming into my life as my student. I am thankful for him teaching me patience. I am also grateful for being able to become more open-minded, more understanding, more loving of other human beings and less judgmental toward them. Perhaps I will meet Corey again in my lifetime. Or maybe I will never see him again. My only hope is my teaching and prayers helped change Corey for the betterment of his life. Thank you, Corey, no matter how you feel about me. I don't hold any grudges, and I am not angry at you or your parents. I will continue to care about you and love you.

CHAPTER THREE:

MIA

(JOY)

Mia was only four years old when her parents signed her up for Suzuki violin lessons with me. The Suzuki Method is a philosophy of teaching students at a very early age how to play by rote—by imitation and by ear; similar to how babies learn their mother-tongue language. It is a delayed note reading approach which involves the parents attending private and group lessons with their children.

I was fortunate enough to teach Mia for twenty years. Although many of my students have ended up studying music lessons with me for at least ten years, I have rarely taught anyone as long as I taught Mia. I watched her grow up from a little girl to a mature young woman. I got to attend Mia's high school and college graduations.

When Mia was ten years old, she played the violin in a Suzuki group for my wedding. I still have the video recording. I often watch the video of our wedding, and it always brings me much joy and honor to know my very own students performed at our wedding before a crowd of 250 guests. Years later, Mia and her parents asked me to play at her wedding. Mia, her mom, dad, and sister were like family to me.

Mia's family was always exuberant with joy and love. Even when she couldn't find a bright side, Mia was an optimist and always looked at everything through rose-colored glasses. The only time I remember Mia being down and pessimistic was when she discovered her boyfriend was unfaithful. She and her parents were continually complimentary of my teaching. They used the word *gifted* when they referred to me as a teacher. Every year for my birthday and Christmas, Mia and her family remembered me with a gift and card. Sometimes over the years they unexpectedly lavished me with gifts at random times. Mia's parents would invite me to lunch or dinner as their way of thanking me for teaching their daughter. I was not only her teacher, "family" member, and friend to her, but I was also a counselor to Mia. I wasn't a licensed therapist, but many times, I felt I was a therapist to so many of my students and their families as they felt comfortable asking me for advice and wisdom.

I remember the time after her violin lesson when Mia turned to me for answers about her relationship with her boyfriend. I noticed Mia had seemed distressed and wasn't acting like herself during the lesson. She was distracted, and her eyes continually looked around the room at everything but her music. She couldn't stand still. I decided to make the first move by asking her some questions.

"Mia, is everything okay?" I asked. "You seemed bothered by something."

In silence, Mia's face turned to dark red, and her hands dramatically spoke feelings she couldn't always express through words. Mia trusted me enough to share her confidential information, but she was shy and had trouble speaking at first. Finally, she simply said, "I'm upset."

I silently waited and listened for her to utter another word. A minute went by, and I could tell Mia was struggling to find the right words, and I didn't want to interrupt her thoughts. Then Mia divulged her inner conflict.

"I thought I could trust my boyfriend, Brett," Mia revealed. "But I guess I can't."

I listened and thought about what Mia had said about the lack of trust in her boyfriend. I wanted to let her tell her story first before I offered any wisdom or advice.

"What happened?" I asked.

"I caught him going out with another girl," Mia answered. "He's been cheating on me for some time."

Mia had just trusted me with a hurtful, embarrassing secret, so I thought carefully before responding. When I realized there was nothing adequate to say, I simply said, "I am sorry, Mia."

I could see a few tears welling up under Mia's eyelids. "I asked him about the girl. I asked if he was seeing her behind my back, and he lied to me," Mia confessed. "He's been lying to me for a long time."

Again, I waited, speaking only a few words to encourage her to keep talking. It was important for Mia to get all her anger and frustration out of her heart and mind.

Finally, when it seemed she had finished, I said, "I am sorry that happened to you." I placed my hand on Mia's shoulder to comfort her. I could see how badly she was hurt, and I wasn't sure what else I could say to make her feel better.

"I'm angry and hurt by him," Mia revealed. "I broke up with him yesterday."

Mia finally broke down and cried until. I reached my arms around Mia to comfort her. I was her counselor, friend, and "family" member, and I tried to reassure her that Brett wasn't the boy for her. I tried to offer my "fatherly" and "mentor" advice. I wondered if I had given her the best advice, but she seemed to accept my words of wisdom.

"Mia, you're going to find someone who's special and who treats you special. You just wait and see. Trust me on this," I said.

Mia's face looked puzzled and curious by the advice I had given her.

"Do you think so?" Mia asked. "Do you think I will find someone special in my life?"

"Yes, I do believe that," I replied. "I will pray that you find that special someone."

"Thank you, Mr. Cline," Mia said. "You are so kind to me."

Mia was seventeen years old at the time, but as I predicted, six years later, Mia met an amazing, loving, and caring man, Lawson, whom she fell in love with almost at first sight. Lawson would do anything for her. He loved Mia deeply. I got to know Lawson well, and he and Mia asked me to play the violin for their wedding. To me, that was the ultimate compliment. Lawson was a fun boyfriend and a fun person to be around. He always teased Mia in a playful, loving way with a dry sense of humor. Lawson made Mia laugh, and he was the perfect boyfriend and husband for her.

I feel like no one comes into our lives by accident. I believe everyone we meet enters our lives for various reasons. Some of the reasons we see immediately, and other reasons we don't learn about until later in life. I have witnessed this phenomenon over and over again. I also believe that people and situations come into our lives to prepare us for something or someone we encounter later in life. So, it is possible that Brett, Mia's ex-boyfriend, came into Mia's life and broke up with her for a reason. Brett was not the right boyfriend and likely would not have been a good husband for Mia, but Brett's entrance into Mia's life prepared her for her future boyfriend and husband. The same thing is true about all the students and their families who have come into my life. Every one of them has prepared me for the future students I would teach, but also, they have prepared me for victories or troubles up ahead. I always marvel at how preparation works in our lives.

Talk about meant-to-bes. Mia and her family came into my life for different reasons, and I believe I was a part of their lives for various reasons. My wife, children, and I had reached a point where we had stopped attending church or would church hop from Sunday to Sunday, searching for the "perfect" church. For those searching for the perfect church, there is no perfect church. The church is like a hospital to help us all recover, heal, mature, love, grow, and become more like God in human and spiritual qualities. Without judgment on us, Mia and her family invited my wife, children, and me to attend church. At first, my wife was reluctant because she didn't know Mia or her family well. She would tell me that they were my friends and not hers. I always replied that my friends were hers and her friends were mine. I encouraged her to try to attend one service, at least, and if she didn't like it, we could stop going. Finally, my wife and I decided to accept their invitation.

Not only did we fall in love with the church members, but our children were also both baptized there, and we ended up attending the church for fifteen years. This church was somehow different from all the other churches we had attended. At first, we couldn't put our finger on why this church was different from the rest. After visiting for a while, my wife and I decided we were attracted to the genuine love and compassion the church family showed us. It wasn't a superficial, fake love, but an honest, sincere love that drew us to them. These people walked the walk in love instead of simply talking. Also, Lawson became an assistant pastor at this church and grew into an excellent preacher.

Our baby girl might have never been healed and saved from her almost-fatal affliction if I hadn't met Mia and her family. When our daughter was eleven years old, she became very ill from a ruptured appendix that became dangerously toxic. She would have lost her life if it weren't for the strong faith, prayers, and love the members of our church exhibited. The pastor was a caring, genuine, faith-strong, and loving man. He always prayed and believed our daughter would be healed and would recover. Also, I will always remember how the church members regularly brought us cards, gifts, and meals until our daughter healed and was able to come home from the hospital. Some of the members even came over to our house and cut our grass while we spent our days at the hospital.

A few years after their wedding, Mia and Lawson had two precious girls. Mia thought highly enough of me to ask me to teach her youngest daughter Suzuki violin. This is only one example of the blessing I have of being asked to teach the child of one of my former students (second-generation student). Her youngest daughter, Bryce, started violin lessons at four years old, just like her mother did. I felt like someone had turned back the hands of time and that I was teaching young Mia again.

I sincerely believe Mia and I were meant to meet and these life occurrences were supposed to happen just the way they did. I am genuinely grateful to Mia and her parents for coming into my life, and I am thankful to God for allowing that to happen. I learned so much from Mia, perhaps more than she ever learned from me. Sure, I helped her prepare for recitals, auditions, and concerts, and I counseled her as a friend. But Mia showed me the true meaning of unconditional love without condemnation or judgment. She gave me so much joy in my life while I knew her.

She helped me learn how to be more optimistic and trust in and rely on God for his wisdom, love, and grace even when it didn't seem like there was much hope. So, in a sense, Mia gave me a whole lot of hope when I was searching and needing encouragement. Mia helped me to return to church and experience a deeper relationship with God. And Mia helped me trust God with my daughter's healing and recovery. I can never repay Mia and her family for all they have given me. Thank goodness Mia left me with fond memories of her and her family. I will never forget her.

CHAPTER FOUR:

ZANE

(EMPATHY)

Zane was like a foster child to me, and though I was only Zane's piano teacher, I also became like a big brother and possibly a father figure to him. Zane started piano lessons with me at age ten because his dad said Zane needed music lessons to help him to improve with his academic studies. Zane's father had heard about the studies that showed improvement in language and numerical scores by taking piano lessons. His dad hoped that studying piano would help his son. His father overlooked the fact that Zane had severe attention-deficit/hyperactivity disorder. Later Zane was diagnosed with ADHD. Still, I have found that my students diagnosed with ADHD and ADD have benefited tremendously from studying private music lessons. The lessons have helped my students concentrate and focus on their schoolwork. The musical studies have also helped my students improve with their memory and their test scores and grades.

I rarely got to meet Zane's father as he was always busy and too preoccupied with other things to be involved in Zane's life. It seemed that Zane's father worked 24/7. I am not sure what kind of job he held, but it was challenging to try to reach him through email, text messages, or by phone. I got the feeling that Zane's father expected others to parent and train Zane instead of himself.

Zane's older sister, Jennifer, was more of a mother to him, and she brought Zane to my home studio for his piano lessons. Jennifer was so dedicated and devoted to Zane. It was almost as if Zane were raising himself and had no family members to care for him, other than Jennifer. Jennifer did the best she could to tend to Zane, but she was preoccupied with taking care of herself as a young woman. In reality, it wasn't Jennifer's job to assume the role of Zane's mother, but she did her best to provide a motherly influence for Zane while he was growing up.

Later, I learned that Zane's estranged mother abandoned the entire family when Zane was three years old. Zane and Jennifer were hush-hush about their mother, never mentioning a word about her or what she was doing now. One day, when I met Zane's grandmother, I learned that Zane's mother had run off with a drug dealer and was "hopelessly" addicted to heroin. She hadn't shown her face or communicated with Zane, Jennifer, or their dad in years. Did that make me think any less of Zane or his sister because of what their mother did? No. I also didn't judge or condemn Zane's dad. Did that make me judge and condemn Zane's mother? No. I never knew the whole story about her and her troubling addiction.

I wasn't nosy, and I didn't want to pry into the family's affairs because it was none of my business. However, knowing more about Zane's family helped me to understand Zane and find new ways to help him. It was good that Zane's piano lesson was the last lesson of the day, usually on Fridays at 5:30 p.m., because Zane was starving for attention and needed some human interaction from a father, brother, or a friend. Zane expressed his hunger for acknowledgment by always calling attention to himself through disruptive behavior.

Since his was the last lesson I taught, I could spend more time with him. After his lessons, Zane hung out at the house sometimes until 7:30 or 8 p.m., chatting and telling jokes. Occasionally we would put on baseball mitts and throw the ball to each other. Fortunately, I have a loving, kind, and understanding wife who was patient. My wife understood that I was trying to help Zane and positively influence him.

Jennifer was shy and rarely said a word. Either she was an introvert or was still carrying deep hurt and resentment around with her from being abandoned by her mother. While Zane and I hung out, Jennifer would sit in the waiting room of my studio and text on her phone. Time spent with Zane gave me great joy, knowing I was helping and nurturing Zane in ways his own father seemed unable to do.

At one point in my relationship with Zane and his family, his dad, who was already financially struggling, called me on the phone. He was emphatic about what he said to me.

"Zane's going to have to quit piano lessons." His voice was a dry monotone.

I paused for a few seconds, surprised and disappointed at this news, and then responded. "I'm so sorry. May I ask why?"

Zane's dad spoke almost immediately. "I'm scraping by, and they cut my hours at work. I can barely afford to put food on the table," he said.

I could tell Zane's dad was telling the truth and that he didn't have the money. Zane would often show up for his lessons dressed in the same worn-out shirt and ragged jeans. When Zane came to lessons, his hair looked as though he had never washed or brushed it. Zane's dad and sister drove beat-up cars that were at least twenty years old. The cars sounded like they were ready for the auto graveyard, and I could often hear their worn-out mufflers and engines from several blocks away when they headed toward my house.

I thought about what answer I would give to Zane's dad when he said he could no longer afford music lessons. "I'm sorry to hear that," I said again. "Would you be open to me giving Zane a scholarship?" I asked.

The phone went quiet for a moment, and I thought he had hung up on me. Then Zane's dad replied, "A scholarship? For what?"

"Because Zane has a lot of promise and potential on the piano," I answered.

I wasn't sure if my answer was sufficient for Zane's dad or if he would accept my offer.

"I don't know about any scholarship now," his dad said.

It was clear that Zane's dad had a lot of pride and wasn't into receiving "handouts." Probably my words about a scholarship had hurt him because he was struggling to provide for his son and daughter. It was never my intention to make Zane's dad feel bad or to hurt his pride. I had offered Zane a scholarship because I sincerely believed in Zane's talent. And I knew how much piano lessons would benefit Zane in many other areas of his life.

I didn't force the scholarship on Zane's dad but let him decide what to do. I offered to teach his son for free. I don't say this in a bragging way or to make myself look good. I honestly wanted to help Zane because I believed in him. I didn't want any praise or glory for helping him. Finally, after a week, Zane's father called me back. His voice seemed excited, different from his usual dry monotone.

"Okay, I've decided to accept your scholarship offer for my son," he said.

And that was the last I heard from Zane's father. He never said thank you or that he was grateful for the scholarship. But that didn't matter to me. It is easy to love people who love you in return. It is much harder to love people who don't show love to you. Never once have I ever regretted the scholarship offer I made to Zane's dad. I continued to teach and spend time with Zane to help him with the little time I had available.

After a year of teaching Zane, my wife and I decided to invite Zane to church. He showed a great deal of interest in church and had asked me several times if he could go along with us. I wasn't exactly sure as to why Zane asked me to take him to church. I got the feeling Zane had ever been exposed to any kind of religion since he was curious about what went on in the Lord's house and what it was all about. I told Zane I would let him experience worship and fellowship, and he could decide if it was right for him. I was careful not to force my beliefs on him and to let him make his own decisions. So, my wife and I picked up Zane at his apartment across town at nine a.m. and took him to Sunday school and the worship service. After church, my wife and I treated Zane to lunch and then took him back to his apartment. We weren't sure whether he would like the church or not, and he didn't say anything on the drive home, so we waited to see his response. My wife and I were okay either way on his decision.

On Friday, when Zane attended his piano lesson, the first words he said were, "Could I go to church with you again?"

I was surprised, and I paused for a few seconds in silence, thanking God that Zane had enjoyed himself in Sunday school and with the worship service. I was eager to see Zane pursue his religious experience.

"Sure, Zane. My wife and I can pick you up at nine a.m. at your place," I replied.

Zane's eyes lit up like Vegas neon lights. He could hardly hold back his zeal about getting to go back to church the very next Sunday. Zane could see the joy on my face too.

"Good, I can't wait," Zane said.

Zane's face continued to glow like a thousand fireflies in the dark. I was delighted to see him so full of joy at the thought of going back to church. So, I asked him, "What did you like about church?"

"It was fun and made me happy," Zane replied.

Although his answer was vague, his response was good enough for me.

That was all I got out of Zane. I didn't force our conversation and just let it all unwind naturally. I didn't know if he genuinely liked the music, the worship, and the people, or if Zane was so hungry for attention that any place where other people congregated made him happy. Or perhaps it was the company of my wife and me and the lunch we treated him to that attracted him to church. It wasn't for me to question his motives. Zane loved to go to church, and he continued to go with us without us even asking him.

I ended up spending more and more time with Zane by taking him to concerts and fun events. Many times, Zane would beg to come over to our house after church and spend the rest of the day hanging out. I could tell my wife and our children's patience were wearing thin with me. They tried to understand that I was helping this attention-starved, lonely kid, but I could tell by their remarks and body language that they were feeling jealous and neglected. Zane was truly becoming like a foster child to me, or perhaps Zane thought of me as his older brother. The trouble was that the more attention I gave Zane, the more he expected from me.

Call it a blessing or a curse, but one day Zane disappeared. He didn't show up for his piano lesson. I called his father, but the line was disconnected. I emailed his dad and tried calling Jennifer, but I never located them. It was one of the most bizarre things that had ever happened to me. I drove by Zane's apartment and knocked on his door, but there was no answer. I learned later from their neighbor tenants that Zane's dad, Zane, and Jennifer moved out of their apartment in the middle of the night. No one had any answers as to their whereabouts. It made me wonder if they were running from something or someone. Perhaps Zane's father was being protected through the US Federal Witness Protection program. Maybe the names they used weren't their real names. Anything's possible, but I never received an explanation for the whole thing.

To this day, I still wonder what happened to Zane, Jennifer, and their dad. I never saw anything on the news about their disappearance, and as hard as I tried to get information as to their whereabouts, the harder it became to track them down. My only hopes and prayers are that Zane and his family are safe and that somehow, during those two years I taught and befriended him, I was able to instill positive values in Zane. Hopefully, I have influenced Zane as a role model and will positively affect him throughout his life. Is that too much to ask? Are those requests wishful thinking? Maybe or maybe not.

One thing is for sure, Zane taught me a whole lot about showing empathy and giving unconditional love. I learned to be patient with Zane through his bouts with ADHD and to be patient with his dad and Jennifer. I learned to love Zane and his family even if they didn't show me the same kind of love in return. I loved them even when they didn't seem grateful for what I had given them. This experience taught me how important it is to try to understand how others are feeling and what might cause them to act as they do. As I said earlier, it is far easier to love people who show us love back.

I gained much empathy during the time I spent with Zane. I learned to try to sympathize and understand what Zane, his dad, and Jennifer must've been going through at the time. And I learned how to sympathize and understand what my wife and children were feeling at the same time. This experience taught me how to become more generous and less selfish with time and money. Zane and his family suddenly leaving without any warning could have been a blessing in disguise because it gave me back more time to spend with my wife and my children. It strengthened our family relationship at home and brought us closer together. But it could have been a curse at the same time because perhaps Zane and his family were in some kind of trouble or danger. I always wondered what happened to Zane and his family. I still pray for their safety and welfare to this day, assuming they are all alive and safe somewhere.

It has probably been twelve years since I last saw Zane and his family. Zane would be about twenty-two years old now. I wonder what he is doing now. I pray that I made some difference in his life. Zane sure made a big difference in my life. I am blessed because of him and am truly grateful.

CHAPTER FIVE:

DANIEL

(PERSEVERANCE)

I met Daniel for the first time when he was only four years old. His mom and his reluctant dad signed him up for Suzuki violin instruction at a preparatory school, under the umbrella of a university where I taught private music lessons. Daniel was a soft-spoken and shy Asian-American kid. He was adorable with his wavy, charcoal black hair and round face. Daniel had difficulty concentrating on his lessons, as typical four-year-olds usually do. His eyes were all over the place, and he had trouble focusing on the violin. At times, he was uncooperative, which frustrated his mom and dad. There were a few times during his lessons when Daniel threw some temper tantrums. Those fits embarrassed his mother and father.

Daniel's mother, Tracy, was a calm, patient woman from Thailand. She was gentle and kind toward her son and toward me. Tracy was eager to see Daniel succeed in Suzuki violin, and she believed in him so much that it showed in every encouraging and positive word she spoke and through her face, which always beamed like the noon sunlight.

Daniel's father, John, was the complete opposite of his wife. John was a tyrant and a retired Marine sergeant who used an automatic wheelchair due to near-fatal injuries he received while serving in the Vietnam War. John spoke with a harsh and dictatorial voice, and if you didn't know him well, you would swear he was a rude and mean man. But there was a lighter side to John. He could crack jokes and laugh about funny situations in life, and every once in a while, the kindness of his heart shone through. Still, he was an intense man and spoke with authoritative command.

I remember one tense moment when Daniel was still four years old. I was trying my best to teach Daniel in a violin lesson, how to play "Mississippi Hotdog" (a variation of "Twinkle, Twinkle, Little Star"). Daniel was stubborn and uncooperative. He threw his body on the floor, screaming and crying, in front of Tracy, John, and me. He kicked his legs up into the air and pounded his fists against the wooden floor. The tantrum was one of the ugliest temper flare-ups I had ever witnessed from all the kids I had ever taught. Suddenly, Tracy and John got into an intense argument over whether Daniel should continue learning with me or not. It was as if Tracy and John were throwing their tantrum too.

"That's it. I've had all I can take from you, Daniel," John shouted with a loud, rough voice. "Pack up your violin. This will be our last lesson, Mr. Cline."

I was stunned by John's reaction to his son's tantrum. Did he realize his son was only four years old? Students that young can sometimes be unpredictable in their behavior. I believe Tracy was stunned too.

"Hold on a minute. Don't I get a say in whether we stay or quit?" Tracy piped up with a heated voice.

"No you don't, Tracy," John snapped.

John's words ignited a firestorm. I silently stood by and allowed their fight to blaze. I was stunned and at a loss for words. I was appalled and saddened by this behavior from Daniel's parents.

Tracy stood her ground and firmly supported the belief that Daniel should continue to study the violin. She believed Daniel was going through a stage and was immature because of his age, but she felt Daniel had talent and wanted him to get an early start and not wait until later. On the other hand, John was vehemently opposed to Daniel taking violin lessons any longer. John believed that Daniel was wasting everyone's time and that he should be allowed to be a kid without being forced to take violin lessons. John and Tracy heatedly argued for over fifteen minutes in front of Daniel, which, in my opinion, was the worst thing they could have done because it caused more damage than good. I believe this negativity led to Daniel's nonchalant attitude toward his violin for a few years after the argument.

I later learned that their argument almost led to a divorce. Tracy won the argument (if there is any such thing as winning a fight you carry on in front of your children), and the two allowed Daniel to continue violin lessons with me. It would take a whole lot of work from me to undo the damage done to Daniel. I worked extra hard in the years to build up Daniel's self-esteem with positive words and praise, and I worked on nurturing Daniel to become an outstanding violin student who wanted to play the violin regardless of how his parents felt.

Daniel turned out to be one of my most gifted and talented violin students. He participated in all of my recitals and concerts and toured with my Nashville Suzuki Players violin group for fourteen years. Daniel also won some important auditions to become a member of several well-known youth orchestras. He turned out to be a top academic student through his hard work and intelligence. At his high school graduation, he was valedictorian, having graduated with a perfect 4.0 GPA. I would like to think that Daniel's violin study, recitals, and concert tours helped him to become the excellent academic student he was. I would like to think I was able to influence Daniel positively through my teaching. I am glad that Tracy stuck to her firm belief that Daniel could become highly successful at the violin and that John gradually became more open to his son taking violin lessons with me. Perhaps my teaching contributed to his welfare, model citizenship, and academic excellence. Or maybe I was only a small part of his success.

Regardless of whether I was able to have a positive influence in Daniel's life, I can say without a doubt that Daniel changed my life for the better. He played an essential part in my life by teaching me many valuable lessons.

Daniel taught me how much effort it can take to drive another person to achieve. He also showed me how difficult it is to motivate and build up someone's self-esteem after he has been knocked down. Daniel challenged me and my teaching methods in ways I had never been challenged before. He strengthened my tolerance and increased my ability to extend my patience to others, like how God continues showering his grace on us even when it seems impossible for him to do so.

Perhaps most of all, I learned the value of being persistent in encouraging a student. I believed in Daniel's potential, and I could see Daniel had great talent on the violin. I could see the big picture of Daniel successfully performing on stage long before Daniel or his father could envision it. Tracy had an innate ability to see the big picture too. She had enough faith in her son that she believed Daniel could be very successful with his violin studies.

It's almost like how God can see the big picture of our lives and knows what we will be before we can see the potential in ourselves. I had this innate instinct about Daniel's potential during the first year he studied lessons with me. Daniel and his parents taught me how important it is in life to encourage others to accomplish goals that they don't believe they can ever achieve. In a sense, you could say I had a strong faith in Daniel, and I did everything I possibly could to encourage him to persevere in his violin lessons. I believed in Daniel so much that I did everything I could to talk his dad out of quitting music. Daniel, John, Tracy, and I became good friends over the years, and I felt I was a part of their family many times. They were always loving, kind, and generous to me, and they showed their appreciation for my teaching with words of praise and through gifts.

I remember a fond memory of their generosity—a random act of kindness during my students' concert tour performances at Disney World in Orlando, Florida. My group, the Nashville Suzuki Players, was invited to perform several live concerts at Disney World and SeaWorld. After our show at Disney World, my students, their parents, and I dined at an expensive French restaurant inside one of the Disney parks. We were seated, and I ordered one of the lowest-priced entrees on the menu. I didn't have a lot of money at the time, and the expensive restaurant would have busted my budget. After we were served and finished our meals, the waiter brought everyone a check, except for me. I told the waiter that there must have been a mistake that I didn't receive a check. The waiter left the table and then returned with what I thought was my forgotten check. And even though I ordered the lowest-priced entrée on the menu, I knew the check would still be expensive. So, I took a deep breath before the waiter handed me the check. But then I was entirely caught by surprise.

"Someone paid for your dinner," the waiter announced with a smile.

I paused for a second in disbelief, thinking something was wrong and replied, "Paid for? What do you mean 'paid for'?" I asked.

"It's free today," the waiter answered.

"Free?" I asked. "Did I win the lottery?"

The waiter chuckled at my humor and replied, "Someone paid for your dinner. I am not at liberty to say who paid for your meal."

I smiled, but my face must still have shown my confusion.

"Thank you," I replied.

The waiter smiled, and before he walked away, he answered me, "Have a wonderful day."

As I sat there at the table, I was curious as to who would have paid for my dinner. Why would anyone want to remain anonymous? I thought long and hard as the parents and students were laughing in conversation. Three names popped into my head. Those were the only three people who could have possibly bought my dinner and wished to remain anonymous: John, Tracy, and Daniel. Even though they never owned up to it, I knew, without any doubt, John, Tracy, and Daniel were responsible for buying my dinner that day at Disney World. That was the kind of people they were. Their love and generosity still affect me to this day and give me many reasons to pay it forward to others with random acts of kindness. I am genuinely grateful to you, Daniel, for giving me the opportunity and honor of teaching you. Persistence and hard work definitely pay off in many ways.

CHAPTER SIX:

LIZZY

(COMPASSION)

Lizzy was a first for me in my long career in teaching. I met Lizzy seven years ago at the university where I was teaching applied violin lessons. I had *never* trained anyone on the violin or any instrument who was visually impaired. Lizzy was born without eyesight, totally blind, and she was a late bloomer on the violin. The university accepted her at the late age of thirty-eight to study voice. When I met Lizzy, I also met one of the most significant teaching challenges in my entire career.

The security guard escorted her to my studio for her first violin lesson because the only device she had to help her find her way was her cane. Lizzy was a cheerful woman and never wanted anyone to feel sorry for her because of her blindness. Lizzy had this special gift of humor, and she could make others laugh while she entertained herself at the same time. When we first met, she told me all about her life and how she was born blind.

"So, have you ever taught a blind student violin before?" Lizzy asked.

"No, I can't say I have," I answered.

Lizzy laughed at my answer. "So, I'm your experiment, huh?" she joked.

"I don't know if I would put it that way," I replied.

While I couldn't look directly into Lizzy's eyes because her eyes were completely shut, I could see what Lizzy was communicating with her facial expressions. Her smile always gave her away, particularly because of her large dimples that appeared whenever she reacted humorously.

"Well, if you've never taught a blind student before, then I am your experiment," Lizzy said teasingly.

"If that's what you want to call it, an experiment, then so be it," I said.

At that point, we both burst out laughing because she knew she could tease me and get away with it, and I knew I was vulnerable because this was completely new territory for me. Lizzy's smile on her round face complemented her sandy-blonde pixie haircut, and she was jovial and usually told a joke or two at each lesson. I admired her persistence and determination. I had no idea what I was doing and how I was going to teach Lizzy. I needed some prayers and a miracle.

I started her first lesson placing the violin up on her shoulder and helping her recognize what the instrument felt like in the playing position. I put the violin bow in her hands and set her fingers in their proper places. It was more about how the violin and bow felt than the usual visual approach I had used so many times before with my other students.

I had to change my entire teaching method to tailor it to Lizzy's specific needs. I learned how to adapt to her disability one step at a time. While Lizzy learned the violin from me, I was taking notes from her lessons about what worked and didn't work. I can't believe that I took the visual part of my teaching for granted all those years and depended on it for so long. Teachers get so used to a particular way of teaching or doing things that they can't always see other possibilities. So, you could say that while Lizzy's eyes were completely shut, my eyes opened wide to all the possibilities out there. Her disability gave me new hope in my teaching of other students with disabilities. I began researching and trying all types of ideas and teaching methods to help Lizzy. Lizzy and I discussed the possibility of using braille musical notes to teach her, and I even considered writing a music method book in braille.

Lizzy had a tool that came in handy in teaching her. She had a voice-activated recorder on her phone, which helped her with recording her practice assignments and her schedule. She also used it to record her violin lesson. Audio recordings of Lizzy's violin lessons became beneficial in helping her make rapid improvement. Lizzy had a super-advanced ear and could hear what many people with eyesight couldn't. Lizzy's intuition, insight, and sensitivity to musical tones and pitches were highly developed. I was amazed at how she could hear a whisper or a very high or low pitch at a very far distance away. I learned how far I had to go with developing my ear to hear what she was hearing.

Sometimes, Lizzy became frustrated and angry at herself for not being able to play the correct notes or create pleasant-sounding tones on the violin. I always encouraged her and told her how much I admired her for having the courage to learn the violin, which is considered one of the most challenging instruments to master. There were times when Lizzy threw a few fits in protest when she was not able to accomplish a goal as fast as she wanted to. Sometimes she became very impatient. But if I put myself in her place, I am sure I would be frustrated and anxious like she was.

Lizzy later confessed to me that her lifelong dream had been to learn how to play the violin. She always loved the sound of the violin and had dreamed of playing the instrument since age three.

Over the next two years, I taught Lizzy; I developed a violin teaching method tailored just for her. While her eyesight was gone, Lizzy's touch and hearing were highly developed, and I built my teaching method around her strengths. Lizzy learned what it felt like to place her violin correctly between her shoulder and collar bone. She learned the muscle memory of holding her violin bow correctly in her hands. Lizzy memorized the feel of each finger against the fingerboard and learned to match the correct pitches with her fingers through her impeccable ear. Muscle memory worked well for Lizzy and served her purpose. I was in awe of all Lizzy was able to learn on an incredibly difficult instrument like the violin.

The violin is a challenging enough instrument to play well for anyone, but to not be able to see what you're playing is an even more difficult challenge. Slowly, but steadily, Lizzy and I both learned together. She was able to complete three books in two years by practicing hard and employing a great attitude. I was impressed; I hardly could contain myself. Her accomplishment was a victory for her and me. Lizzy graduated from college, and as far as I know, she is now teaching voice in a school on the west coast. I hope and pray that I have positively helped Lizzy and given her what she needed for her life.

One thing I know, Lizzy taught me a lot about life. I thought I knew what patience was until I met Lizzy and began teaching her violin. I must confess that there were times when I felt as frustrated as she did. I lost sleep researching late at night, trying to learn how to teach Lizzy effectively. Sometimes, Lizzy and her violin studies consumed my thoughts and much concerned me. I sincerely believe that some people or situations come into our lives to equip us and help us to prepare for jobs later in life. Lizzy taught me how to be infinitely patient, no matter what challenge came my way. Life doesn't always go the way we think it will, and life doesn't always cooperate with our plans. I learned to be adaptable, with an open mind, to each situation in life no matter the circumstances. Lizzy's joy and positive attitude taught me to make the best of any case, and if you think you have it wrong, take a look around and see someone who has it worse. Lizzy used her humor in a valuable way, and it always made her forget her worries at the time. Her humor made her challenging life a little easier.

Although Lizzy didn't want me or anyone to feel sorry for her, I learned a lot about compassion from teaching her. I admired the way she didn't grumble or complain, even on her worst days. She remained cheerful and full of joy despite frustrations that come from living blind in a visual world. I didn't appease Lizzy or try to humor her; I treated like any other human would want to be treated. I showed her love, kindness, and respect. Soon, Lizzy was not only my devoted student but also was a faithful and loyal friend. Sure, I had to adapt my teaching method to accommodate her disability, but I never acted like I felt sorry for her or made her feel like I was giving her special treatment. I still expected Lizzy to practice hard and to achieve the goals I set for her. Inside my heart and mind, I tried to put myself in her place and tried to understand how hard each day might have been for her with her disability. The opportunity to teach Lizzy indeed increased my compassion and gave me the empathy I needed to exhibit with others and situations ahead in my life. Lizzy prepared me for life's challenges in the future.

I also learned from Lizzy the true meaning of determination. Sure, my musical training in college gave me courage and discipline. And I learned that to be successful at something, I had to be persistent and consistent. But teaching Lizzy gave the word *determination* a whole new meaning for me. Despite all odds against Lizzy learning how to play the violin well, she overcame each one of them, step by step. It wasn't easy, but with patience and determination, Lizzy was able to learn how to play with excellent intonation, the right tone, and accuracy of notes and rhythms.

Lizzy's success story could indeed be a book in itself. She continued learning the violin with fierce persistence while others who did not have her challenges to overcome might have given up a long time ago. Never once did Lizzy use the words "I can't" or "I quit." Those words weren't in her vocabulary. I am amazed at how determined she was. Her fortitude gave me new hope to go the distance and know I can accomplish anything in life if I set my mind and heart to it.

I am so grateful to Lizzy for teaching me the valuable lesson of compassion. I felt like a new and transformed man and teacher after my experiences with teaching Lizzy. I pray that God will continue to bless Lizzy wherever she is now, in everything she does in life. God has indeed blessed me by bringing her into my life. I only hope I was able to teach her something during the two years I knew her.

CHAPTER SEVEN:

LOUIS

(FORGIVENESS)

I had the opportunity to teach another student with disabilities, but this time on the guitar. I never imagined myself teaching students with disabilities. And sadly, I had missed out on so many blessings in the past by not keeping my mind open to the possibility that God might want me to teach this special group of students. The Presbyterian Church in town asked me to teach Louis at a brain rehabilitation center. So, I traveled each week to the center to help Louis learn acoustic guitar. Louis was a sweet, kind gentleman of fifty-four years of age. He was tall, distinguished, and wore his gray hair short.

I remember Louis proudly telling me he qualified to become a member of Mensa. For those who aren't familiar with Mensa, it is an organization that inspires and empowers intellectually gifted people to make positive contributions to society. The minimum requirement for acceptance into the prestigious group is a score of 132 or higher on the Stanford-Binet IQ test or within the top 2 percent of the population on comparable tests.

Since Louis scored an IQ of 164, that put Louis in the top one percent. No one had to tell me Louis's IQ score; I could tell when he opened his mouth. He was highly intelligent with an advanced vocabulary and sharp memory. His achievements were quite impressive, particularly for someone who almost died of a massive brain injury. Louis was so well read that he could recite entire books as if he had a photographic memory. Unfortunately, sometimes Louis had so much knowledge in different areas that he would start chatting in the private music lessons and get carried away. I had to respectfully reign him in by developing a balance for him in his music lessons. I realized I couldn't allow him to take his entire thirty minutes each week to talk to me about everything he had learned about a random topic. So, I learned to politely listen to what he was saying for a few minutes and then gently steer him back to playing his guitar. It was a delicate balance I had to learn.

After about a month into teaching Louis guitar, we became comfortable enough in our relationship for him to open up and reveal his story. One day, after his lesson had ended, Louis shared with me the devastating details of how he ended up at the brain rehabilitation center.

"I used to live in Virginia," Louis said.

"That's where I was born and raised," I replied.

"I used to be the manager of What-A-Burger in Winchester, Virginia," Louis continued.

"I know where that is. I lived in Richmond for twenty years," I said.

"One night, about seven years ago, I was closing up the store late after finishing the books," Louis said. "It was a beautiful night, not a cloud in the sky. All the stars were visible."

I sat on the edge of my chair, with great anticipation yet dreading to hear what was about to come.

"I whistled a happy tune as I walked toward my car," Louis said. "There wasn't a soul around as What-A-Burger was on a lonely stretch outside of town."

I couldn't stand the suspense building up inside me, waiting for Louis to get to the heart of his story. Louis was flamboyant when he told a story, and he would drag every detail out until he finally arrived at the part you really wanted to hear.

"All of a sudden, out of nowhere, these two hooded thugs swinging baseball bats jumped out from behind my car and began beating me with their bats," Louis said.

"God, that is awful," I replied.

"I screamed and shouted at the top of my lungs, but no one heard me," Louis continued. "But by then it was too late. They had left me lying on the blacktop for dead."

Louis's story was too much to absorb. I couldn't imagine that kind of brutality happening to anyone. I paused a moment before asking, "Were you unconscious?"

"No, miraculously, I was still breathing, but barely," Louis confessed. "The thugs had beaten my brains out, and I was bleeding pretty badly."

Again, I needed a few seconds to come up for a breath. It was a compelling story, and I needed time to digest it. "How in the world did you live to tell this story?" I asked.

"Fortunately, an employee happened to drive by, hoping he could still catch me inside What-A-Burger. He had left his wallet inside the store and came back to try to find it," Louis said.

"Wow, he was like your guardian angel," I replied.

"You can say that again. I owe it all to God for returning Randy to the store at that very moment," Louis confessed. "If it weren't for God and Randy, I would have died. Randy called 911 on his cell phone when he found me lying in a pool of blood in the parking lot. The paramedics rushed me to the University of Virginia Hospital Brain Trauma Center. My brain had swollen to twice its size in a matter of minutes. The surgeon cut the top of my skull completely open to relieve the pressure from the swelling."

"Unbelievable," I replied.

"Yes, it is unbelievable," Louis confessed. "I call it a miracle. The surgeon worked on me for fourteen hours to keep me alive."

"Sounds like you had a mighty good surgeon," I replied.

"Yes, Dr. Klaus is one of the best surgeons in the world, and of course, UVA hospital has one of the best brain trauma centers in the country," Louis revealed.

All at once, Louis's memories became emotionally too much for him to handle. Louis's face flushed red with pain and anguish. The muscles in his face tightened up as a flood of tears flowed down his cheeks. I sat quietly and placed my hand on Louis's shoulder to comfort him as he was revisiting probably the most painful memories of his life.

"God saved my life, and I owe it all to him," Louis said. His voice quivered as he choked up with more tears.

"You are truly a walking miracle," I replied. "Surely, God has some great plans for you since it wasn't your time to go."

"Yes, and I believe God has some great plans for the two guys who attacked me."

His response startled me because I wasn't expecting Louis to comment positively about the two thugs who nearly killed him. I had to pry further.

"How so?" I asked.

"Just as God showed his grace and mercy on me, I showed my grace and mercy on those two boys," Louis answered.

Again, Louis gave me an answer I was never expecting. I had to absorb his words before I could continue. "Seriously?" I asked.

"Yes, the police finally caught the sixteen-year-old boys and were going to charge them as adults for attempted murder," Louis revealed.

"How much time did they get?" I asked.

"None. I decided against pressing charges because it would have destroyed those boys for the rest of their lives."

Now Louis had thrown me completely off guard. I thought about what Louis said and how he could drop charges against two people who attempted to take his life. I responded slowly, "But they almost killed you."

"As ruthless and merciless as those boys were, leaving me for dead in the parking lot, and as difficult as it was for me, I decided to forgive them," Louis revealed.

I sat on the edge of my seat in silence. How could Louis have forgiven and forgotten what those boys had done to him? How could Louis have rid himself of all the anger and bitterness he must have felt over the struggles and difficulties he faced because of what they had done to him? How could Louis have so much joy and contentment in his heart as he has now? I was curious to find out what drove Louis to forgive his attackers.

"How did you learn to forgive those boys and forget what they did to you?" I asked.

"I realized I couldn't keep that bitterness and anger inside my heart forever," Louis admitted. "All that bitterness and anger would have eaten me alive, and I certainly wouldn't be alive today if I hadn't forgiven those boys."

I took a deep breath because all Louis was saying was very deep for me to understand.

"I never thought of it that way, Louis," I replied.

"You see, God is the only one who judges," Louis said. "I will let God decide what he does with those boys."

Louis's answers produced many thought-provoking questions in my mind.

"Do you know what those boys are doing now?" Louis asked.

"I have no idea," I responded.

He smiled like he was about to share a delicious secret. "Both of those boys have turned their lives around. Both of them went on to graduate from high school and attend college. One of the boys is a successful paramedic technician who saves lives, and the other is a park ranger for the Blue Ridge Mountain State Park," Louis proudly stated.

"That is amazing, Louis," I replied. "You gave those boys a second chance with their lives."

"Yes, thanks to God," Louis said with a humble tone.

I learned so many lessons from Louis as my student and friend. Hopefully, I was able to give Louis something in return as his teacher and friend. Louis taught me so much about what it means to forgive someone truly. I learned that as hard as it is to do, we must forgive someone if they have done us wrong, no matter how bitter and angry we feel. I learned that if we harbor bitterness and anger in our hearts, it will kill us with some disease or wear our bodies down. I marveled at how Louis was strong enough to forgive those boys who nearly killed him and not hold any anger or bitterness toward them. His story and words of wisdom have rung right to me to this day. Whenever I know someone had treated me wrong, I always hold on to Louis's words to reassure me; everything will turn out okay if I just forgive them and forget about how they mistreated me. Louis's words have given me courage and made me a stronger person than before.

Teaching Louis also taught me how to have more empathy and compassion for others. I admired how happy and content Louis seemed to be even though his life had been full of troubles. I learned to be respectful and polite to Louis when he wanted to take his entire lesson up, talking and sharing. But I also learned how to reign Louis in and to be kind about it. I would gently remind him that I was also here to teach him the guitar and that I wanted him to learn all he could from me on the guitar.

Being around Louis made me try to live inside someone else's heart and mind and work to understand everything they are going through. I believe the lessons I learned from Louis about forgiveness have helped me appreciate my friends, family, and students better than ever before.

CHAPTER EIGHT:

JEFF

(LOVE)

If I knew back then what I know about Jeff now, I wouldn't have changed anything. I would have continued to teach Jeff with patience, empathy, and love. Sometimes, people make mistakes that turn their whole lives upside down. In Jeff's case, he made one huge mistake that sent him to prison. I am not ashamed of my student for what he did, and I continue to love him to this day.

I first met Jeff when he auditioned for the youth orchestra I directed years ago. He played in my orchestra for four years, and I got to know him reasonably well. In many ways, Jeff seemed like a troubled kid. He was always seeking attention by disrupting the orchestra, talking, or showing off with his flashy trumpet skills. Jeff knew how to divert attention to himself and to distract others from learning. I would correct him numerous times, and he would just smile at me with an innocent look as if he never did anything wrong. Jeff knew how to push my buttons. He pushed a lot of others' buttons too. It wasn't fair that Jeff would distract and steal time away from the other students who were there to learn. I am sure they resented his disruptive behavior.

It was as if he enjoyed annoying me because he liked me and thought he could get away with it. I did like Jeff and tried to do everything I could to help him. Jeff was a decent trumpet player, and I figured if I could praise and encourage him, perhaps he wouldn't need so much attention in the orchestra where he was disruptive and wasted everyone's valuable time. I tried praising and encouraging him, but it seemed like that wasn't enough for Jeff. The more I appreciated him, the more he wanted my attention. I realized after a while that I couldn't be his babysitter. Nevertheless, I continued to show my love to Jeff.

I learned later from his parents that Jeff had a rough life. These revelations explained why Jeff behaved the way he did and why he sought so much attention. Jeff and his brother were adopted from single parents who had criminal histories and were unfit to serve as parents. I must mention that Jeff's brother played trombone in my orchestra, but his brother was the quiet, shy type and didn't show any behavioral problems. Perhaps, his brother thought about calling attention to himself but was too shy to carry out his temptations.

Jeff and his brother were removed from their biological parents due to the abusive treatment they received. They were both severely beaten and, at the same time, neglected. Both parents were arrested for selling and using illegal drugs and were involved in other illicit criminal schemes. The brothers spent several years in foster homes while waiting for someone to adopt them. No wonder Jeff was seeking so much attention in the youth orchestra by being so disruptive. He was merely crying out for someone to love him. Jeff was starving for affection from all the years he had been shuffled around between his parents and among foster homes. Jeff's current parents adopted him at a late age of eleven years old.

My heart broke, and I was saddened when I heard Jeff and his brother's story, and it made me want to do everything in my power to help the brothers succeed. Many of Jeff's habits had already formed by that age and were difficult to change or break. In many ways, Jeff didn't know how to love because he had never experienced genuine, unconditional love from anyone until he was adopted by two amazing, sincere, and loving parents. Even if Jeff's teachers, parents, and I showed him real, unconditional love, I am not sure Jeff would have recognized what real love was. And I am not sure at the time whether Jeff and his brother were ready to accept genuine, unconditional love from anyone. It would take years to undo all the wrongs and injustices Jeff and his brother had suffered during their many years of abuse and neglect. Unfortunately, Jeff and his brother knew only their abusive treatment over their childhood years and had a jaded view of the human condition.

I continued to show my love for Jeff. I tried to guide and steer him toward working hard to achieve his goals, staying out of trouble, finishing high school, and going on to college or a trade school of some sort. I began to grow close to Jeff, and gradually Jeff learned to trust me and worked hard for me in the orchestra. Jeff no longer tried to seek attention in the orchestra, and his behavior improved because he was applying himself to becoming an ace player. After his high school graduation, I lost track of Jeff and his brother. I thought I would never hear from him again until I got the dreadful news from his mother.

Jeff's mother called me with an anxious, quivery voice. "Mr. Cline, Jeff is in some big trouble," his mother said.

I paused for a moment and took a deep breath, dreading what I might hear.

"I am so sorry. Is there anything I can do to help?" I answered.

"Maybe. Jeff was arrested on Tuesday and is awaiting a hearing with the judge." His mother's voice sounded highly distressed, and I could tell she might cry.

I was careful not to ask his mother what crime the police accused Jeff of and any other details. I let her do the talking, and I listened. She paused in silence as I could hear the frustration and hurt in her voice. I could also hear the sobs and could only imagine her eyes welling up with deep emotions she couldn't express at the time.

"What can I do to help?" I asked.

"Jeff's attorney says he needs some letters of reference from those who knew Jeff. Could you please write a letter on behalf of Jeff?" she asked.

"Sure, I'd be glad to help. When do you need my letter?" I asked.

"I'll need it by next Wednesday," she answered.

"Okay, I will get a letter written in support of Jeff," I replied.

"Thank you so much. You meant so much to Jeff. He always looked up to you," she said.

"Thank you. That is so kind of both of you to say. I will do everything I can to help," I replied. "My thoughts and prayers go out to you. I know it must be a difficult time for you right now."

"Thank you," she said. "It is a difficult time."

Jeff's mother hung up the phone, and a million questions flooded my mind. I went on with my teaching during the day, but my mind was distracted by the troubling news of Jeff's arrest. I had never had a single student arrested and accused of a crime. I was overwhelmed with mixed emotions and felt helpless for Jeff.

That evening, I turned on the local news to discover Jeff's name all over the headlines. My jaw dropped, and my eyes grew twice their size as I sat frozen on the edge of my seat to hear the devastating news. The news reporter said police accused Jeff of raping a twelve-year-old girl. My student of four years who played in the youth orchestra was facing charges of rape—and rape of a minor. The news was difficult and troubling for my mind and heart to process. Without judgment, my mind sorted out the most important questions to ask. Could Jeff have committed the crime he was accused of by his victim? If he had indeed committed this crime, what would have been going through his mind when he did it? What would make Jeff commit such a crime? I was confused and at a loss for words because I had no concrete answers. If my student had indeed committed the crime and was convicted, he would serve a long time in prison. My heart went out to Jeff and his parents and the young girl and her family. I prayed for all of them without judgment or condemnation.

I wrote the letter of reference for Jeff based on what I knew about him in my early association, and I sent it to his mother. Weeks later, Jeff stood in front of a dozen jurors without showing any emotions on his face and heard the foreman's authoritative voice announce the verdict: "Guilty." Jeff's mother and her husband buried their faces into their hands and wept uncontrollably. My student was found guilty of raping a twelve-year-old girl.

I was stunned and stood in my tracks frozen when I heard the shocking news from the local TV anchor. Instead of worrying about what would happen to Jeff and his parents, I began praying for their strength, comfort, and wisdom. I also prayed for the victim and her family. I prayed for resolution, healing, forgiveness, and for the victim and her family to start rebuilding their lives.

A week later, I learned that since this was Jeff's first offense in his life, the judge sentenced him to eight years in a maximum-security prison. While I am sure the victim and her parents felt this was a light sentence, Jeff's parents were devastated that their son would be going to a maximum-security prison for eight years.

From time to time, I would send Jeff cards and notes of encouragement while he served time in prison. The judge sent him to Riverbend Maximum Security Prison in Nashville. Riverbend is considered one of the most high-tech penitentiaries in the United States for its innovation in technology.

Even after a year later, I couldn't get Jeff off my mind. I thought about him and what he was going through in prison almost every day. I contacted his parents and asked them what I could do for him. They suggested that I could visit him one day soon. We arranged a meeting date, and his mother and father picked me up in their car and drove me to the prison. I was highly anxious; my knees shook, and I fidgeted with my hair and face. I had never visited a prison before, and I didn't know what to expect. On the way, his mother thanked me for visiting Jeff and told me how much it meant to him that I was coming to see him. She described the rape of the girl in detail and how it happened. His mother told me more graphic information than I cared to know. I was surprised she would open up to me and tell me every detail.

We finally arrived at the prison, and after showing our IDs at the gate, we entered the prison with caution. We all had to surrender our personal belongings and be scanned by an X-ray machine. Next, we stepped through a solid, metal door that must have been eighteen inches thick. We watched the heavily armed guard shut and lock the door behind us. We walked down a long corridor until we reached an open area that resembled a cafeteria called the common area. The guards directed us to sit at the table in the center of the room, perhaps designated for visitors. Armed guards stood all around the room at the entrance and exit points. The prisoners, dressed in their bright orange jumpsuits, congregated at the tables around us as they ate the prepared lunches from their plates and trays. Jeff's face lit up when he saw us, and his smile was wider than the state of Texas as he sat across from us at the cafeteria table. It appeared prison life had been hard on Jeff as he had put on an extra forty pounds, and he was slow of thought and speech.

"I am so glad to see you, Jeff," I exclaimed.

"We have missed you," his mom said. "We think of you and pray for you every day."

Jeff's dad remained reserved and speechless. I got the feeling that even though his dad loved his son, he felt uncomfortable in that situation. I wasn't sure what was going through Jeff's father's mind. I tried to put myself in his position and imagine what he must have been going through.

"See that guy over there, the one with the long black sideburns?" Jeff said. "He was on the news recently for stabbing his wife and two children to death."

Jeff seemed to be more obsessed and preoccupied with the prisoners around him than he was with us. He knew the criminal history of each of the prisoners in the room. Jeff told us what crime each one had committed and how long they would stay there.

No wonder Jeff had gained a lot of weight. The food looked gross and high in calories and carbohydrates: mashed potatoes, meatloaf, gravy, biscuits, and cookies. Jeff told us he was only allowed to go outside thirty minutes a day to play basketball.

Even though it didn't seem like Jeff was in the mood to talk about what was going on in his life or how he felt, I am sure he appreciated our visit. I am sure our visit meant more to him than we will ever know. We were only allowed thirty minutes with Jeff, but I will never forget those thirty minutes spent in prison with him. I felt anxious and somewhat paranoid, looking over my shoulders, thinking a prisoner could overtake a guard at any minute and that my life was in danger. But I am glad I faced my fears and biases and visited Jeff.

Years later, Jeff was released from Riverbend but had to wear an ankle monitor. I reached out to Jeff and his parents to see what I could do to help him get back on his feet again and make the tough transition back into society. My wife and I hired him to do some landscaping work, and we kept in touch with him as Jeff gradually made his transition. Later, he was registered in the public records as a sex offender, but I still tried never to treat him differently, only to love him.

I am not sure whether I taught Jeff much during the time when he was a student in the youth orchestra. Perhaps time will tell if I made any impact. Jeff never really did anything with his trumpet or music. But then again, only a handful of music students go on to become professionals or to even study music beyond high school. That is okay because it aligned with my teaching philosophy of music. I believed that I was always teaching students to love and appreciate music, not to make them become professionals. Some did become very successful at music and are making a comfortable living. Two went on to become famous in the commercial pop music world. There are so many benefits to learning a musical instrument, as studies prove. Music strengthens the language and mathematical skills of the learner. Music improves academic scores, it improves right-hand/left-hand coordination, and it helps a student become a more organized and disciplined person. I have read that there are at least a hundred benefits to studying music.

Whether Jeff learned anything useful from me or not is inconsequential at this point. I most definitely learned much from Jeff. He taught me how to endure patience with someone over a long period. Jeff taught me how to encourage and mentor students even when they weren't students of mine anymore. I believe a teacher doesn't just teach a student for a specific amount of time and then forget them. I think a teacher can be a mentor to their students and continue shepherding and guiding them through life long after their students have left them.

Jeff taught me how to become more empathetic to others around me. After I learned Jeff's tough background and how he had been tossed from his parents to foster homes until the age of eleven, I put myself in Jeff's mind and heart, trying to understand all he had gone through that made him who he was. I tried to understand all the feelings and thoughts Jeff felt. He made me a better teacher and a better human being because I learned empathy.

Most importantly, Jeff taught me the meaning of unconditional love and how to apply it with others in everyday life. I learned to never give up on someone even if we think they have failed themselves and us. There is hope around the corner, and if we keep loving a person through all their failings and mistakes, love will overcome it all in the end. I never gave up on Jeff. I always loved him through all his mistakes and poor judgments. This understanding of unconditional love and patience has helped me deal with other stressful situations in my life with students.

I am grateful for God bringing Jeff into my life. I am thankful to God for allowing me to experience the challenging life Jeff lived. Jeff's life of hardships has prepared me to teach and mentor other students effectively. Wherever Jeff is today, I pray that he has straightened his life out and is doing something meaningful in this world.

CHAPTER NINE:

ROXIE

(PASSION)

I had rarely seen a kid as creative and passionate about music as Roxie. Roxie's mother, Gracie, signed Roxie up for private piano lessons at age seven at a music store where I was teaching in Nashville. Although DNA and being born under musical parents doesn't necessarily predict the musical success of a student, in this instance, I believe it did. Gracie was an avid and talented singer-songwriter in the Nashville area and was the single mother of Roxie. Gracie was also Roxie's biggest fan and stage mother to her. Maybe it had to do with the lofty dreams Gracie had failed to accomplish at the age of forty or because Roxie was Gracie's only child. For whatever reason, Gracie did everything she could to propel Roxie's music career.

I remember how hard it was to teach Roxie traditional or Suzuki piano lessons. She fought me and resisted playing traditional classical music throughout the time she studied with me. I tried everything possible to make her lessons fun and to motivate her to practice the classical songs, but she finally won. I believe it was the independent streak in her and the rock-and-roll blood in her veins that made her such a rebel. I decided not to fight Roxie with her staunch resistance to learning classical music. Fortunately for her, I was not one of those teachers who rigidly go by the book when teaching piano. I believe that my background of writing and performing pop and country songs helped me to become more open-minded about teaching creativity. I allowed Roxie to write her songs on the piano and express herself through her voice in singing her songs. Little did I know that I was developing a pop star, and literally, a star was being born. I remember how gifted Roxie was at age seven. Her melodies, harmonies, rhythms, and lyrics were advanced and mature for her age. I recognized her gift and potential and encouraged Roxie every step of the way.

By the time Roxie was ten years old, she had performed her original songs with voice and piano for songwriter's rounds and on radio and TV shows. In three short years of lessons, Roxie had become an excellent singer and songwriter. By the time Roxie had turned thirteen, she had developed a cult following. Her fans came to every one of her concerts and practically worshiped Roxie and her talent. Her accomplishments made me proud, and her mother's face was beaming from ear to ear.

As much of an independent spirit as she was as a little girl, Roxie became even more of a rebel and lived a rogue life after losing her mother to a fatal aneurysm when Roxie was thirteen years old. Roxie's aunt raised her until she turned the legal adult age. I can't blame Roxie for her rebellious, wild, and rogue life. She was angry and frustrated with life, and she carried around her pain from unexpectedly losing her mother. Living without her mother as an adolescent was extremely hard on Roxie. While her aunt was family, she would never replace her mother.

It was so sad Gracie tragically died when Roxie turned thirteen, and Gracie couldn't see the fruit of her encouragement, patience, passion, and hard work with her daughter.

I had encouraged Roxie to cultivate her gifts of songwriting, performing on the piano, and singing until she was eighteen years old. Roxie decided against majoring in music in college but did graduate from high school before her singing career took off in a big way. Roxie ended up becoming a rock star and signed with Arista Records, a major record label. Roxie signed with a major entertainment manager and toured with such greats as Aerosmith and Kiss. Roxie's dreams were becoming a reality in a big way. While it pains me sometimes to know Roxie wasn't able to show her mother the culmination of all her efforts, I was thrilled beyond anything I had ever felt before because I had worked hard to develop Roxie's talent, and I had never had a student who had achieved so much in such a short time with their music.

Although the lifestyle Roxie led as a rock singer, continually touring on the road, wasn't the lifestyle I would have chosen, I continued to encourage and mentor Roxie through her rockstar accomplishments even after I stopped teaching her at age eighteen. Roxie was living the dream only a few people ever achieve, and at an early age, she was using the gifts God gave her. I was proud of Roxie for using her gifts and making something of herself. I am sure her mother is smiling down from heaven at all her daughter's achievements, and she is cheering for all of Roxie's accomplishments.

While I may not have had much influence on Roxie and her life, I gave her my best as her teacher, as I have always given to all of my students. I allowed her to be expressive and creative in writing her songs. I encouraged Roxie to push herself to write to high standards and to work hard to continually improve her piano playing and singing. Whether I made a difference in Roxie's life or her career is debatable, but I know Roxie made a significant difference in my life. I always admired Roxie's fiery passion for her music since the early age of seven. During the eleven years I taught Roxie, she remained passionate without waning in her love of piano performances, songwriting, and singing.

I was amazed at how prolific Roxie was in writing songs. She could write several complete, outstanding songs in a week, and her memory was impeccable. She taught me what it took to become enormously successful in any field or career—passion and drive. Roxie possessed both of those qualities, and I am sure that is why she is so successful today. She was able to combine her natural gifts with her passion, drive, and persistence. She was so persistent that she continued to press on with her writing and performances no matter what others thought of her talents. Roxie didn't care what others thought; she knew she was gifted, talented, and was going to be a star. Roxie was right in her instincts, and she taught me much about believing in myself, regardless of what others think about me.

I am thankful to God for bringing Roxie into my life. I am proud of her and all her accomplishments and grateful for all I have learned from teaching and knowing Roxie. I only wish her the best through all her endeavors in life. Rock on Roxie.

CHAPTER TEN:

ELIJAH

(MOTIVATION)

If you told me a famous superstar music recording artist would hire me to teach his four-year-old son violin lessons and that the superstar himself would be bringing his son to the lessons, I would probably tell you to keep on dreaming. But that is what happened. I met Elijah for the first time when his father brought him to my home studio to study private Suzuki violin lessons with me. The music superstar dad sat in on the first lesson as well as the other lessons, as is required by parents in the Suzuki method. I took a deep breath, relaxed, and acted cool around Elijah's dad. I treated him with respect, courtesy, and kindness as I would any other of my parents. I was my complete self and didn't try to be anyone other than myself. I never once showed Elijah's dad any special treatment just because he was famous. Also, I didn't allow myself to become paralyzed by intimation. My daddy always taught me that everyone puts their pants on the same way, and everyone bleeds the same regardless of whether they're famous.

Elijah was a cute little fellow, chubby with sandy-blond hair. He started learning on a tiny violin that resembled a toy. Elijah's father was so proud of him, and I believe he could see a budding star in his son. Unfortunately, Elijah didn't practice as he should have, and it took a lot of work to motivate him to practice. Of course, Elijah was only four years old at the time, and it has always been difficult holding the attention of that age group for very long. Elijah's mom and dad were disappointed but continued with lessons, hoping that things would change and that Elijah would gain some interest. Elijah ended up sticking with the violin until he was fourteen years old. At that time, Elijah lost interest in music and traded his violin for football to play with his high school team.

Despite the fact that Elijah quit after studying violin for ten years, those lessons were never considered an act in vain. Elijah not only accomplished a lot during that time, but there were also moments when Elijah enjoyed himself. Elijah participated in most of the recitals and group concerts of my popular group, the Nashville Suzuki Players. He toured with my group for live concerts and on TV and radio shows through seven states in the Southeast and even got to perform live on stage at Disney World and SeaWorld. Elijah met a lot of beautiful friends through all of the concerts and recitals.

One moment I will never forget is the time Elijah's dad invited my Suzuki violin group to perform live on a large TV network with him.

"I would like for you to arrange my song for your group to play with me when I sing onstage," Elijah's dad requested.

"I would be honored," I replied.

"This will be a wonderful opportunity for your students to perform on TV before a huge audience," Elijah's dad said.

"I am excited about this opportunity. Thank you," I said.

Elijah's dad seemed pleased that I was so appreciative and enthusiastic about my group performing with him on live TV.

My group worked on the song for the longest time and perfected it until we could do a dress rehearsal with Elijah's dad. We probably participated in over twenty rehearsals before our TV debut. I remember the day of the TV performance in front of a live audience. Everyone had to arrive early for makeup and to warm up and tune up. All the kids were nervous with their hands and knees shaking and the palms of the hands sweating profusely. This was my students' big international debut on a popular TV show that aired around the world. Over one hundred million viewers watched the show weekly on seven continents. My students had performed on local TV for the news and news-type shows, but this would be our most massive audience ever.

You should have seen the starry-eyed faces of my students as they stood there on stage before a live audience in the bright lights next to a superstar singer with television cameras pointed at them. The parents, before and after the show, were so nervous and excited for their kids.

They couldn't sit still, and many of them paced the floor behind the stage and perspired before their children went on stage. I tried to remain calm and collected, but underneath my cool demeanor, I was a nervous wreck. My knees shook, and my stomach felt as if it was going to explode. I worried that something could go wrong and that perhaps either my students or I could have a memory lapse and forget the songs we were playing.

The producer of the show gave us a thirty-second warning. Then he counted down to one and pointed his finger at our group to begin. The red record lights on the cameras flashed while the interview and the live music started. This was a proud moment for everyone. I couldn't believe how well my students performed. I breathed a deep sigh of relief and was ready to relax. All our hard work and persistence had paid off in the end. I was awestruck over how my students excelled and shined through that nervous, stressful performance.

After the show was over, my students celebrated. They knew how well they had performed, and it built their confidence, not to mention how much it motivated them. I could finally sleep at night.

This show launched the visibility and fame of my group, the Nashville Suzuki Players. We started receiving invitations to perform for dignitaries and celebrities all over the place, and it led to us eventually being invited to perform at Disney World. This television show launched a major tour of the Suzuki Players of seven states in the Southwest. Those were some exciting times and some highlights of my teaching career. About six months later, my group was invited to perform in a World War II veterans video. We recorded in a professional recording studio in Nashville and shot the video at a local Nashville university. The video ended up being aired on CMT TV network and other networks all over the country and resulted in my group being nominated for a Grammy award. I never dreamed that my group would be nominated for a Grammy award! And even though we didn't win, it was a huge honor just to be nominated. There were thousands of groups just like mine, doing the same thing I was doing, and yet our group was nominated for this prestigious award.

So, you can see how many fun opportunities Elijah got to experience before he quit violin although these opportunities might not have seemed so new and fresh for Elijah since his father was a superstar. More importantly, perhaps, the addition of Elijah to my class opened doors and opportunities for my other students who may never have had those experiences. I must say his decision to discontinue playing the violin was disappointing. Sometimes that happens. You'd think that Elijah would have been highly motivated like the other kids and would have wanted to participate in more of these exciting events, but apparently, they weren't for him. Sometimes, you teach a kid for a long stretch at a time, and you think that kid is going to follow a path in music. Then he decides to do something completely different from what you expected him to do. It's hard to know what to say when those students throw you a curve and surprise you by stopping their lessons. Nevertheless, my work with Elijah was not in vain, and I hope that maybe he learned something from me or perhaps that I might have had some influence on him, which might show up years from now.

I gained a lot of knowledge from teaching Elijah. It took a whole lot of patience to motivate him to get excited about music and keep him going on the violin as long as he did. Sometimes the work was exhausting, but the rewards were great. Teaching Elijah reminded me why I was teaching in the first place—to pass along the love of music and not necessarily to make professionals out of the kids. I learned that there are events or happenings in teaching that you don't see coming or are difficult to predict. Also, I learned to work comfortably around parents of students who are celebrities. I learned that they are no different than you or me. They achieved fame from their hard work, blessings, and luck, but when you strip away their celebrity status, underneath, they are often regular Janes or Joes just like all the rest of us.

Elijah taught me how to encourage even when encouragement didn't seem possible. You have to always keep a positive attitude and wear a bright, friendly smile on your face even when the sky is falling all around you. I learned more about how to be patient, how to motivate, and how to encourage my future students from teaching Elijah. It also helped me to devise successful teaching strategies, games, and tools to use for many of my students.

Motivating students to practice is one of the greatest challenges for music teachers. We have so much to compete with today, such as video games, tablets, smartphones, social media, TV, movies, and streaming channels. We as teachers practically have to be illusionists, magicians, performing what might seem impossible in order to light fires under students who are undermotivated. I gradually learned what made Elijah tick. I tailored my teaching strategies around Elijah and his interests. This valuable knowledge I learned from Elijah's needs helped prepare me for future students I would teach who were similar to Elijah in temperament, personality, and character.

I am very grateful to Elijah for coming into my life. I am grateful for his dad and mom for providing some wonderful performance opportunities for my Suzuki violin group. Elijah brought with him many wonderful blessings and chances for my students to get to perform in venues they would never have experienced otherwise. I hope and pray that someday Elijah and I might reconnect and that I might be able to learn more about how music possibly affected his life in a positive way. If that should happen, it would be a blessing, but if not, I still would have learned so much from Elijah and his parents. Thank you.

CHAPTER ELEVEN:

TINA

(HARD WORK)

Tina was the cutest little girl I had ever seen. At age two and still in diapers, Tina resembled a doll with her pink complexion, round face, short dark hair, and a floral dress that hung past her knees. Tina's violin was the tiniest one any of my students had studied with, as it was a 1/32 size. Violin companies don't make violins any smaller than that, and it was the perfect size for Tina's petite frame. I wondered how my teaching of Tina would turn out and if she would continue with me for the short term or for the long run.

Tina's dad, Sam, was Tina's biggest fan. Sam assumed the role of "stage dad" from the day Tina picked up the violin. Sam must have recorded over ten thousand videos of Tina in her lessons, in concerts, recitals, and everywhere she performed throughout the more than twenty years I taught her. Sam was a proud daddy, and he wore that proud, wide, papa smile on his face everywhere he went. He also attended every one of Tina's violin lessons until she could drive herself to lessons in her own car. Sam played guitar really well and would accompany his daughter every time she performed. He was patient with Tina up to a certain point, but you could tell he expected so much more from her potential and talent. While I was trying to teach the love of music, Sam had a much bigger plan in mind. I didn't realize until later on how far Sam wanted to take his daughter with her talent.

Tina made huge advancements in her violin playing and was able to reach level seven out of the ten levels by the time she had reached sixteen. Tina, however, wasn't interested in finishing the last three books. Bluegrass fiddling was her passion, and she wanted to pursue it in a big way. Tina became interested in playing fiddle by age seven, and her daddy started entering her in fiddle and bluegrass competitions. Sam took Tina to competitions all over the country, as far away as Idaho. Tina's very young age placed her at a disadvantage because she was not advanced enough to win a competition, but the competitions weren't fair in the fact that there was no cut-off age for competitors. In other words, Tina was competing with adults who were way more advanced and more experienced. But as Tina grew older, she became more experienced and proficient on the fiddle.

One particular bluegrass competition drew Tina's eye year after year: the Smithville Jamboree. This jamboree has drawn audiences of over one hundred thousand each year and is still aired live on PBS-TV.

Tina and her dad would enter each year from the time Tina was seven through fifteen, but she would never win an award or even place. But on Tina's sixteenth birthday, everything was about to change. Tina and Sam practiced furiously and put in long hours of fiddling in preparation for the annual July event. I'll never forget the call I received at the end of that day.

"Mr. Cline, we have some big news to tell you," Sam announced, his voice high with excitement.

"You won the jamboree?" I guessed.

"Tina not only won the jamboree, but she beat them all!" Sam shouted.

"What do you mean? I don't understand," I said.

"Tina won the grand championship prize for the whole jamboree," Sam exclaimed.

I couldn't believe the news I was hearing. I was elated and wanted to throw my hands up and do the happy dance.

By that time, Sam was unable to contain his joy and enthusiasm. His voice had peaked at a fever pitch, and I could tell he was about to explode with joy and happiness as he shared the details of Tina's performance.

"That is unbelievable," I replied. "Her hard work and persistence finally paid off after trying to win for nine years."

"She is so thrilled because she won $10,000 and a gigantic trophy," Sam exclaimed.

"I am so proud of Tina," I said. "Congratulations."

"Tina is following in the footsteps of the best. Mark O'Connor and Alison Krauss won this same award years ago," Sam said.

"I am so impressed," I replied. "We'll have to celebrate!"

And sure enough, Sam took my words about celebrating literally. The next week, Sam and his wife treated me to a very nice dinner, where we celebrated with Tina for her grand championship award.

Tina and her dad gained a lot of mileage out of the grand championship win. Tina was featured in newspapers, magazines, and on local and statewide TV shows. I believe that her winning this award was the turning point in her career and musical studies. Her win was responsible for her receiving multiple offers of full-ride scholarships to some really good colleges. And Tina was in high demand as a fiddle player. People hired Tina left and right to perform at weddings, appear at special events, and to play at bluegrass concerts. She could have chosen to attend any college of her choice, but instead Tina chose to go to the university where I was teaching. While I was flattered and honored that she chose me as her teacher in college, I was not sure if it was a good and healthy thing to do. Tina felt comfortable around me as her teacher and friend, but she probably needed to get other perspectives and learn from other teachers in order to advance in the violin and fiddle. She had already studied with me for sixteen years; nevertheless, she was now determined to study under my tutelage for another four years on the violin.

When Tina graduated from college and announced she was getting married, I was so humbled and honored when she asked me to play the violin at her wedding. She could have chosen any violinist in Middle

Tennessee to play her wedding. Nashville is full of excellent violin and fiddle players. But Tina chose me to perform.

After Tina's graduation and her wedding, Tina moved to a city located about three hours from Nashville to start a teaching and performing career of her own. It was sad to say goodbye because Tina and Sam were like family to me. We were really good friends. I had watched Tina grow up out of diapers and into a young lady. I watched her drive when she got her license, win a major fiddle competition award, graduate from college, and get married. A whole chapter had closed for both of us, and it was sad for me to move on from that chapter in my life.

I hope and pray I was able to make a positive difference in Tina's life. And even if I had only a small influence on Tina, she taught me so much about teaching and life. It took a great deal of patience to teach the violin to someone in diapers at age two. I had to remain patient with Tina's overzealous dad, who, at times, tried to do the teaching instead of me. I had to be patient and flexible when Tina decided she loved to play fiddle tunes more than she loved playing classical music.

Tina and her dad taught me how determination and hard work pays off with the violin, fiddle, or with anything in life. Tina struggled to remain positive and not give up when she didn't win any award or competition for nine years. Her hard work of practicing finally paid off in a big way at the end of the ninth year when Tina was awarded the grand championship trophy and $10,000. That's determination. Tina and her dad had laser focus on that trophy for nine years. That's all they talked about, and that's what they practiced toward winning. Tina and her dad remained optimistic about winning and achieving their goal even after years of disappointment. If they got a little down or discouraged, it was only for a day or less, and then they were back on their feet again, chipper and enthusiastic about trying to win.

I will always remember Tina and her dad. I am grateful they came into my life. I believe that Tina was my longest running student in my teaching profession. I am thankful Sam chose me as Tina's teacher and never stopped believing in me. It was a long, productive journey of twenty years, and I learned so much from that adventure. Thank you, Tina and Sam, wherever you are.

CHAPTER TWELVE:

GABBY

(COMPASSION)

Gabby was a high-needs student who had a disability that made it difficult for her to accomplish her goals and dreams. I met Gabby when she was nineteen years old. She came to me requesting that I help her with her songwriting and piano studies. Gabby was scattered and had so many talents and interests that it made it difficult for her to focus on any one thing. I didn't learn about her disability until after I had been teaching her for a while. It was only then that I realized the challenges that lay ahead for my work with Gabby.

Gabby signed up with me for three hours of private instruction per week. Normally, most students only study thirty to sixty minutes of lessons a week, depending on the age of the student. I had never had a student sign up for more than sixty minutes of lessons per week. I later learned that everything Gabby did was extreme to the point of obsession. It was either all or nothing. I began to wonder how she would pay for her music instruction with me and if she could afford to pay me $180 a week. But she always came through. Gabby's parents both worked steady jobs as a veterinarian and as a pediatrician. Her parents didn't mind paying for Gabby's music instruction. They believed they were investing in their daughter's education, particularly since Gabby had dropped out of college and had plans of her own to become a hit songwriter, concert pianist, singer, actress, model, and other interests she would dream up as she changed her mind from week to week. Basically, I went with the flow and tried to encourage Gabby to focus on one or two of her talents instead of hopping from one interest or dream to another.

As hard as I tried to reign Gabby in at each lesson, much time was spent on the outlandish and absurd conspiracy theories and wild beliefs she would share. I politely listened and became her "therapist," too, but I knew Gabby's parents didn't want me talking about one-world governments and how a certain intelligence group was out to get her when I was supposed to be teaching Gabby music lessons her parents were paying for. Certain elements of peculiar, paranoid talk increased in Gabby's stories and behavior. I hadn't observed that odd behavior in the beginning. Gabby would bring me handfuls of newspaper and magazine articles on various subjects, including "research" on the latest health food or supplements for whatever ails you. I politely accepted Gabby's offerings without arguing or debating with her and took every advantage of the pauses in her conversation to steer her back to piano and songwriting lessons. Sometimes I was successful at getting Gabby to focus while at other times, I miserably failed.

When Gabby practiced the piano, she sounded quite good, and she had advanced to the high level of book seven. But Gabby seldom practiced the piano like she was supposed to. Her attention was scattered in too many directions to be successful in any one field. I tried to teach her the principles of successful, commercial hit songwriting. I taught her that less is more in writing successful songs and showed her, by example, that hit songs rarely have any more than two verses, two choruses, and sometimes a bridge. But then she would return the next week with a stack of pages with lyrics. Her songs had at least nine verses, nine choruses, and bridges. What she had written was chaotic with no form, and she rambled without structure. It was as if Gabby had forgotten all I had taught her about how important it is to write with clarity and concision. Gabby was very unorganized in everything: her music, the way she dressed, in her thoughts, and in her conversations. She was very scattered in almost everything. I tried my best to help her become more organized with her music.

Then one day out of the blue, Gabby didn't show for her three-hour private lesson. I didn't receive a call, text, or email explaining why she wasn't there for her lesson. I became worried because it was not like Gabby to fail to call when she wasn't going to make our appointment. I left a voicemail message for Gabby on her phone. After I still hadn't heard from Gabby in three days, I called her parents. They were very secretive as to where she was and didn't want to divulge much information. They made some excuse, saying Gabby had to go away for two months to Atlanta to take care of her ailing grandmother, which didn't seem credible or believable to me. It was almost as if Gabby's parents were hiding some deep dark secret, and they acted ashamed of whatever they were hiding. I almost lost my patience and was ready to give up on teaching Gabby, but something inside me told me to not give up on her. Something told me that I was put there in Gabby's life for a reason, to give some calm and stability to her unstable life.

So Gabby didn't study with me for almost three months, but she did eventually return to study piano and songwriting with me. I accepted Gabby back as a student, feeling like there was a greater calling for me to work with her. I wasn't exactly sure of what that calling was at the time, but I learned later it wasn't all about me teaching her music. When I asked Gabby how her grandmother was, she changed the subject as if she didn't want to talk about it. I didn't pry and went on with teaching Gabby where we left off when she had disappeared twelve weeks before.

Through my ten years of teaching Gabby piano and songwriting off and on, I began to notice a pattern of how Gabby would study with me for perhaps four or five months and then disappear and not show up for lessons for a period of anywhere from one month to six weeks. After a certain point of Gabby missing so many lessons, her parents finally broke down and revealed to me why Gabby had missed so many classes. Gabby was diagnosed with both bipolar and schizophrenia disorders. For those who are unfamiliar with bipolar disorder, a person with this condition generally experiences shifts in mood, energy levels, and thinking. Someone with schizophrenia tends to lose all perception of reality. After Gabby's parents explained to me that their daughter suffered with these conditions, I began to understand her actions and why she did the things she did. Everything made sense. Her parents explained to me that her condition would worsen to a critical point where they had to commit her to a psychiatric hospital because she would experience mental breakdowns. Gabby would spend anywhere from one month to six weeks in a psychiatric ward until her condition would improve, and she would no longer be a danger to herself or others.

So, now you can understand why I opened this chapter with the sentence about Gabby's disability severely impairing her from accomplishing her dreams and goals. Unfortunately, Gabby's condition has worsened since I last taught her. It makes me sad to see her in the lethargic and apathetic state she is in today. Gabby has been committed to a twenty-four-hour assisted living home, where she is monitored and treated with antipsychotic drugs to keep her condition in check. Gabby has no one to take care of her because her mother, father, aunts, and uncles have passed away, and her brother is unable to take responsibility for caring for her.

Despite the fact that Gabby now lives her life in an almost comatose, non-functional state, I don't believe for a minute that my teaching and working with Gabby has been in vain. I believe that I made her life happy by providing music to her, and I gave her hope when hope couldn't be found. Our lessons together helped Gabby reach and strive for her dreams, and that probably brought happiness to her at the time. Music lessons provided structure for Gabby's life when she most needed a stable life.

But what I learned from Gabby was invaluable to teaching my future students as well as to living my own life. Gabby taught me a lot about what it really means to be patient over time, not just being patient for a short time and then giving up on a student. Gabby was my "stop-and-go" student who would attend lessons for a few months and then vanish until she surfaced again weeks or months later. I learned that, without asking for explanations, I could accept Gabby back as my student time and time again for ten years. Gabby taught me how to be patient when she would share her conspiracy theories, the latest health cure, or her other views. She taught me how to listen without judging, criticizing, or condemning. Gabby taught me how to be friendly and listen politely, but she also taught me to know when to reign Gabby back in to stay on the subject matter, which was either playing piano or learning how to write songs.

I learned a whole lot about how to become more empathetic and compassionate. No one knows when a disease might strike someone. A medical condition could afflict us at any time unexpectedly in our lives, sometimes when we are the most vulnerable. In Gabby's case, her schizophrenia and her bipolar disorder began affecting her at the young age of nineteen.

Some people in this world have an odd phobia about or are prejudiced against people with mental illnesses. Basically, it's based on a lack of understanding and education. Mental illness is a disease just like heart disease or cancer, but it affects the brain instead of another internal organ of our bodies. From the current research I've read, many mental illnesses occur when there is a chemical imbalance of the body. Anything internally or externally can trigger an imbalance, such as a poor diet, lack of exercise or sleep, an infection, or another disease. Stress or even something as simple as the changes of seasons can suddenly trigger a bipolar episode. Getting to teach and know Gabby gave me knowledge in the area of mental illness. I learned a lot from reading research studies, articles, and books on mental illness so I could better understand how to relate to Gabby.

With the new understanding of Gabby's prognosis, I was able to grow in becoming more compassionate and empathetic toward her and toward my future students. Gabby taught me to care more, love more, and show more kindness to others than before. I am most grateful to Gabby and her parents for the opportunity to teach Gabby and am especially grateful for all that I learned from her and them. Thank you, Gabby.

CHAPTER THIRTEEN:

JEREMY

(DETERMINATION)

Jeremy was an enterprising young man who was a rising star. He was a homeschooled high schooler when he signed up for violin lessons at the university where I taught in the preparatory school. With a very high IQ, Jeremy was amazingly bright and started studying with me when he was fifteen years old. Jeremy was self-taught on the violin, and by the time he started lessons with me, he was fairly advanced. But he needed discipline, and he needed to be polished. Being self-taught, he played sloppily from the poor violin habits he learned. Jeremy had an impeccable ear and could improvise well, but he wasn't a good sight reader. He was definitely gifted, and his amazing ear for pitches and tones gave him an advantage over other students his age.

From the first day I met him, Jeremy had big dreams. I remember our conversation that very first day.

"I need to know your short and long-term goals so I know how to teach you effectively and help you reach every one of your goals," I said.

"I'm starting an alternative, independent (indie) band. I've got a guitar player, bass player, singer, and a keyboardist, but I still need a drummer," Jeremy replied.

"Sounds awesome," I said. "What do you hope to do with the band?"

"I'm writing songs for our group and hope to tour when we're ready," Jeremy answered. "Hope to attract a label deal."

Jeremy was so business minded. He had his life all mapped out. One of Jeremy's strengths in music was his uncanny ability to arrange and improvise on existing melodies. He could take a popular hit song and suddenly change and enhance the tune until it sounded like a totally new song. His ability was more than just a talent; it was a gift because it came so naturally to him. Jeremy could also sing and play the piano well, both self-taught. After the second year Jeremy studied violin with me, he started a successful band composed of a female lead vocalist, two guitarists, a bass player, a keyboardist, and a drummer. Three years later, Jeremy fell in love with the lead singer of the band and asked for her hand in marriage. I was invited to their wedding and treated as one of their VIP guests.

Jeremy's group went on to tour, showcase, and perform on the East and West Coasts. As of this writing, Jeremy's band is close to signing a major record deal with a well-known recording label. Just as Jeremy had envisioned, one of his dreams was becoming a reality.

I remember our conversation at another lesson.

"I want to start a music school one day," Jeremy shared. "It will be located in Nashville, and I will be the CEO and president of the school."

Jeremy's words felt so real and sincere. It was as if he were speaking from years of experience and wisdom, and he believed every word he said would come true.

"I'm going to hire the best teachers in Nashville, and we will offer first-class instruction in all musical instruments," Jeremy exclaimed. "We will teach students of all ages, and we will have the best practice rooms and concert halls around the Nashville area."

There's no doubt in my mind that when Jeremy receives his business and music degrees next semester, and when he finishes touring with his band, he will open a very successful music school, and it will prosper and flourish. Jeremy has always been a planner and a doer, and mark my words, if Jeremy puts his mind to something, he gets it done.

What fascinated me about Jeremy was that he didn't waste time talking about what he planned to do. He already had it mapped out and seemed to know the route and direction to take to get his dream fulfilled. It was a gut feeling, a natural instinct for him. Jeremy had a level, down-to-earth instinct and good business sense.

Another amazing quality of Jeremy was his ability to know how to prepare himself for what lay in the future. He was not content to earn money from a part-time job that paid the minimum wage when he knew he had a talent that could earn him seven times the amount he would be paid working in retail or fast food. While others his age in high school would be earning seven dollars an hour, Jeremy taught private piano and violin lessons to beginner students at a nearby music school and made $49 an hour. Jeremy became so successful and in-demand with his private teaching that his heavy teaching schedule started to take a toll on his academic studies, his band rehearsals, and his violin studies. Jeremy made more money in one day teaching young students than more high school students would make in a week working their part-time jobs. Call it ingenuity, call it brilliance, but Jeremy was destined to make plenty of money with his dreams.

If Jeremy didn't already have enough to do with his time, he found another way to make lots of money. He hired himself out to play for weddings and special events. Jeremy had the whole business model down to a T. He printed fancy, attractive business cards with flyers advertising his violin performances for special events. He made a very good living for someone of any age, let alone a high school student. Jeremy would receive $300 for a one-hour performance at a wedding, bar mitzvah, or a funeral. I was totally amazed at how Jeremy came up with all these plans for how to earn money part-time using his own gifts and talents. Sometimes his violin practice suffered because he was spending so much time teaching and performing that he had little time to devote to advancing to a new level on his violin. Nevertheless, Jeremy managed to practice his violin enough to receive a full scholarship to the college where I currently I taught. Jeremy is doing very well today and succeeding with all of his dreams. He is making a comfortable living as a young, married man, playing with his band, writing original songs, teaching private music lessons, and performing for weddings and special events.

I am not sure how much he gained from me as his teacher. Jeremy was already naturally gifted and could play the violin in circles around students his age. One thing for certain I do know is that Jeremy taught me so much while I was his teacher. I already knew about hard work as everything I ever earned from birth was from hard work. No one, not even my parents, gave me any handouts. While some teens my age were getting brand-new cars, money, and gifts for having to do absolutely nothing in return for them, I had to do yard work, deliver newspapers, shovel snow, rake leaves, and whatever it took to obtain things others got for free. My parents made little money, and I grew up in poverty. Everything I ever received and earned because of hard work made me appreciate what I had. So I related to Jeremy since he had to work hard for everything he received. Jeremy came from a family of eight children and didn't get any handouts. I still believe hard work pays off and that hard work never killed anyone in life as long as they had passion for what they did. If you are in a miserable, worthless job that causes you undue stress, then, yes, maybe it will shorten your life. It will definitely prolong your life if the work doesn't feel like work at all.

Jeremy taught me what it means to have dreams and ambition. He refused to let anyone tell him he couldn't achieve something in life. The minute someone told him how impossible it was to do something, Jeremy set out to prove them wrong. He seized his dreams and went after each one with drive, determination, and passion. Jeremy was always an optimistic person. I don't ever remember seeing Jeremy down or discouraged. He was so on fire with his dreams, and his enthusiasm was contagious. I learned that if you are passionate about your dreams and work hard, others will see your enthusiasm and will sooner or later jump on your wagon and become a part of your team. I think it is human nature to do so. No one wants to be thought of as a loser or a pessimistic person. That was one of the biggest characteristics I always admired about Jeremy.

Just being around Jeremy for even a little while was motivating and inspiring. Jeremy's positive, can-do attitude caused those around him to want to reach higher and to accomplish so much more than they ever dreamed of. Jeremy was a breath of fresh air for me as I had taught probably five thousand students before I met him, and I can honestly say, hardly anyone came close to motivating and inspiring me as Jeremy did. Thank you, Jeremy. I am truly grateful to have taught you and for all that I learned from you.

CHAPTER FOURTEEN:

AMBER

(COURAGE)

They said it couldn't be done. Many of my colleagues told me I had my work cut out when I accepted Amber as one of my students. Twelve years ago, I taught at a community school located outside of Nashville. I worked there for four years and was able to teach violin, viola, and piano to a good number of kids in the town.

Amber's parents brought Amber to meet me for her first violin lesson. Amber was sixteen years old but had the emotional and mental capacity of a four-year-old. Her parents never revealed her diagnosis, but I learned from the director of the school that Amber fell somewhere between mentally challenged and intellectually challenged. Since I wasn't an expert on brain conditions, I wasn't sure what her learning disability was. All I knew was that she was very limited in what she could do or say. Her parents helped her to walk and with her underdeveloped motor skills. I observed that some kind of abnormality severely disfigured Amber's face, and her hands were shaped almost like claws instead of developed like most hands and fingers we are used to seeing.

I spent much of the first lesson getting to know Amber. I wasn't sure how much she understood from my first introduction, but I did see that I had my work cut out for me in teaching her. I prayed for a whole lot of patience, wisdom, understanding, and compassion, as I was nervous and unsure of myself and my teaching abilities. Sure, I had over twenty-seven years of successful teaching experience, but I didn't have much experience teaching students with disabilities. This new experience shook my confidence. Plus I knew I would need an infinite amount of patience to prepare Amber to play violin adequately. And it was painstaking, indeed, but if given the same opportunity again, I would happily accept Amber or another student with such a disability.

It took weeks to teach a tiny step at a time. I relied heavily on repetition. After I had showed Amber hundreds of times how to hold the violin correctly in playing position, she was able to keep the violin properly on her shoulder all by herself. I considered that an accomplishment, and it encouraged me. Her parents were very patient and were inspired too.

Then came the challenge of learning how to hold the violin bow. Since Amber's hands were shaped differently, it was challenging to teach Amber how to hold the bow in the manner professionals recommend. So I had to adapt a particular bow hold for Amber's hand so she could at least hold the bow securely enough to make a decent sound out of the instrument. Again, repetition was her friend and mine. I must have placed the bow in her right hand over a thousand times so that she got the feel of what a secure bow hold felt like in her hands. There were many times when Amber lost control with her hand position and would drop the bow to the floor. But I always patiently encouraged and praised her through it all. I suggested that Amber and her parents listen to the CD recording of Mozart's first variation of "Twinkle, Twinkle, Little Star," hoping that would prepare her to play the song.

Weeks and weeks passed before Amber was finally able to hold the violin bow securely enough to draw some strokes across the E and A strings. To her parents and me, that was one sweet victory to get to hear Amber play a decent tone on the open E and A strings, this by a student who took over one thousand attempts just to hold the bow without dropping it. I praised Amber up and down for her accomplishment. I am not sure Amber understood why I praised her. To many students, learning to hold the bow without dropping it was a cinch, and most could do it in a single lesson.

Now that we had the bow hold down, I worked with Amber to curl her fingers around the neck and fingerboard of the violin and to curve her fingers so she could place her fingertips against the fingerboard. Amber would require this skill in order to play the notes of her first song, Variation A of "Twinkle, Twinkle, Little Star."

As hard as I tried to get her fingers to curl around the neck and fingerboard, I failed each time. Amber had great difficulty curling and curving her fingers as both hands were disfigured, rigid, and inflexible. Nevertheless, I kept trying and refused to give up. I was determined to teach Amber how to play the violin. I ended up physically placing her left hand around the violin's neck and fingerboard, and I picked up each one of her fingers and put them where they were supposed to go. I probably repeated this physical process a thousand times before moving a finger on the left hand. There were times, I admit, when I had my doubts as to whether Amber could keep her left hand in the correct position long enough to be able to play a song while holding the violin bow with her right hand. But the hard work of repetition, muscle memory, and persistence finally paid off with Amber.

After umpteen-thousand tries, Amber surprised us all one day at her lesson. I nearly fell over backward and almost did a double-backflip when Amber played the notes to the "Twinkle, Twinkle, Little Star" Variation A, holding the bow by herself and placing her left-hand fingers in the correct places on the fingerboard to produce the results. I was astounded, and a wellspring of tears flooded my eyes as I choked up with deep emotions. Amber's parents broke down with tears streaming down their cheeks. And if that was all Amber learned from me in fourteen months of violin, I felt Amber, her parents, and I had achieved a fantastic feat. I felt joyous and victorious that day, knowing we had accomplished what seemed impossible to do.

Unfortunately, I left my teaching position the next year due to being offered an excellent teaching job closer to my home. I lost contact with Amber and her parents and the rest of my students when I stopped teaching at the school, which was eighty miles away from my home. I offered Amber and her parents my best wishes and helped them find another teacher, but I wondered what had happened to Amber years later. I hope I had contributed something to her life by adding the dimension of the violin. I believe I was able to help Amber in some small way, but regardless of whether I helped her, I am genuinely grateful to Amber and her parents for what they taught me.

Amber and her parents taught me how to have an incredible amount of patience. I continually encouraged and praised Amber, even though there were many times I felt discouraged or felt like giving up. Without yelling at her or getting angry, I patiently picked up Amber's violin bow off of the floor when it fell from her hands many times. "You can do it, Amber. I believe in you," I would say.

Amber's parents would smile at me as if to say, "Thank you for believing in our baby girl."

At times, it was an exhilarating experience, and other times I wanted to scream and tear my hair out in frustration. But each time, my patience and endurance grew more substantial from the time before.

The fourteen months I taught Amber taught me a lot about courage. I always considered myself to be open-minded and free of bias and prejudice. Still, I truthfully must admit I was at first frightened by the prospect of teaching a student who was drastically different from any of the students I had taught before. I didn't know how to act around Amber, and I was afraid I couldn't instruct her. But after delving into teaching Amber for a while, I found my work with her to be rewarding, and I was no longer afraid or anxious.

Inspired by Amber's courage, I found the courage to teach her and knew from that moment that I could use that courage with other students who might have profound differences. I am thankful for that gift of courage. Finally, I found a great deal of compassion along the way too. Working with Amber and her parents gave me a considerable amount of empathy, which I only discovered through teaching Amber. This gift of a particular type of kindness made me a better teacher and gave me new strengths and powers I never had before. I could, in turn, utilize these gifts in the future with the Ambers in my life. Thank you, Amber, and your parents for giving me so many gifts and for teaching me so many valuable lessons in life. Wherever you are now, I want to let you know how truly grateful I am to you.

CHAPTER FIFTEEN:

SETH

(CREATIVITY)

When I first met Seth, he was the tender age of five. At that time, I had no idea what a remarkable child he was and all the hidden talents he possessed, which were about to be unveiled. Seth was a talent to be reckoned with.

At first, Seth's mom hired me to teach him the Suzuki violin. I traveled to their house, a quick stop from the school where I taught in Gallatin, Tennessee. Seth became quite good on the violin quickly and performed with my group at local recitals and concerts. I remember Seth's true gift beginning to reveal itself at age seven. Seth wrote several excellent instrumental compositions for my group (violin and piano). My group performed his songs and received a standing ovation for his originality and for his ability to compose such amazing tunes at such an early age.

    The first time I stepped into Seth's house, I noticed some beautiful and original-looking prints and paintings hanging on the walls of their living room. I inquired about the artwork and discovered that Seth's mother was the artist of all of the pictures and prints on display. Seth's mother was a professional artist who had studied at a prestigious university and had received awards for her artwork. This inquiry led to a whole slew of artistic collaborations through my friendship with Seth's mother. My group began recording CDs every Christmas, and we recorded some fiddle albums. Each album needed professional artwork with graphic designs. Seth's mom, Laura, generously provided the artwork for free for all ten professional albums my group recorded in a Nashville recording studio. Laura later drew all of the watercolor illustrations for at least ten of my children's picture books, which were published by a well-known book publisher and distributed worldwide to over sixty countries. Little did I know that teaching a five-year-old student how to play the violin would lead to a fruitful, professional business relationship that would last for years. I consider Laura to be one of the finest illustrators I have ever met or worked with while writing books. She rivals any of the great illustrators in today's best-selling children's picture books. Laura is a master at what she does and has always maintained a positive, professional attitude.

    At age eight, Seth decided he wanted to play the piano. Usually, many kids start on the piano and branch out to other instruments. So I taught Seth Suzuki piano, and he flourished with his playing to such a high level that he began making up tunes on the keyboard. Seth's ear was impeccable. He could pick up any song he heard on the radio, in concert, on TV, or in films and almost immediately perform it. I decided to feature some of Seth's original tunes on my group's albums, with Seth playing them on the piano. Seth's songs were a hit with my students, parents, and those who purchased our CDs.

Then came the drums the next year. Seth continued to play the piano but decided he wanted to learn some other percussive instruments too. He persuaded his parents to purchase a whole set of expensive drums, and they hired a drum teacher. Seth's entire career was unfolding and coming together, and I didn't even see it until much later. Sometimes, it is hard for a teacher to see the big picture his student is imagining until it starts to come together later. Nevertheless, I did allow Seth his creative freedom to explore all the possibilities of his gifts and talents.

After the drums, Seth started writing lyrics with his melodies and began singing his original songs. I helped Seth develop and craft his lyrics and melodies to improve his chances in the highly competitive commercial music industry. Seth continued to improve on his lyric and melody writing until, at the age of fourteen, he attracted the attention of a music producer. This producer saw the vast potential of Seth's gifts and talents in the music industry. He offered Seth, at the age of fifteen, a deal to record his first album of all his original music. His album was a big success after radio and TV shows played his songs, but he still hadn't landed a major recording deal. The producer said Seth needed to carve out a special niche that would make him unique as a recording artist and help him stand out in the crowd. Sure enough, it wasn't long before Seth found his niche. Seth and his parents discovered through their ancestry and DNA that they were all part Native American.

Seth decided to dress the part of his heritage and began learning how to play the double-chambered Native American flute. It was designed in North America by Indigenous people and had a slow air chamber at the head end of the flute. Not only did Seth work on mastering the Native American flute, but he also began to design and carve out handmade flutes, which he offered for sale at his concerts and by mail order. At this point, Seth was a musician, singer, songwriter, inventor, young businessman, and later became an actor. I had no idea how remarkable Seth indeed was with his many gifts and talents. As you can probably imagine, Seth was incredibly intelligent and honored for being in the top one percent of his class in academic achievement. Seth wasn't just talented and gifted; he was a hard worker too. Often, teachers will find that some gifted students rest on their laurels. They know how skilled they are, but they fail to work hard to improve their skills.

Seth carved out an incredibly unique niche for himself in his remaining teen years. I continued to teach him piano and guide him with his songwriting. Seth and I even wrote a few songs together. His parents hired me to play violin and cello on a few of his music albums. The Native American dress, flute, original songs, and acting took off for Seth. His producer was thrilled because he finally found a unique recording artist who stood way out from the crowd, and this producer could now sell Seth to a major record company for a major recording deal.

Suddenly, Seth's career was on fire, and he became well-known via national concerts, TV appearances, and radio shows. His songs were regularly played on the radio, and his videos received many likes on YouTube. Seth had many followers and was building a strong fan base.

As of this writing, Seth has become a very successful recording artist, songwriter, and actor. He has been nominated multiple times for Grammy awards and has reached number one on Billboard New Age charts several times with his songs and albums. Seth has won many prestigious music awards and has been honored multiple times with other accolades, and his most recent endeavors include starring in several movies and TV films as an actor, singer, and songwriter. He has recorded with major symphony orchestras and has co-recorded with some well-known artists. I predict Seth will become a superstar within the next ten years. I am so proud of Seth and the talented, gifted adult he has become.

I suppose only time will tell if I truly made a difference in Seth's life. I have had students contact me many years later to thank me for teaching them and to tell me how much they learned from me. I may hear something from Seth years from now, or I may never hear anything ever again from him. That's the way it goes with teaching. You don't always receive instant feedback or input on your teaching. Out of the thousands of students I have taught, I have perhaps heard from a handful of them. That's okay. I wish every one of them well, and I hope they have learned something from me. I have certainly learned much from each one of them.

Seth showed me how to remain positive, work hard, and create even when you can't always see the fruit of your labor. Seth had many gifts and talents, but the most important one was his ability to see into the future and visualize his possibilities. I always admired Seth's steadfast, unwavering faith, and how he had this uncanny ability to look far ahead and see the big picture on the screen in his mind. This skill of Seth's was brilliant, and I only wish I had seen what he saw in his mind when he was much younger. Seth was dedicated, committed to his dreams, and was one of the hardest workers I had ever met. He was so inspiring to me and motivated me to become a better teacher and professional musician.

Seth also taught me his free use of his creativity in everything he did, particularly in his music. Seth didn't let anything hinder him or get in the way of his creativity. He never felt oppressed or stifled and didn't care what others thought of him or his creative endeavors; he just created. I admired his confidence, enthusiasm, and passion for his music. Seth was always a curious student and was still anxious to try new instruments and new approaches to performing and writing. Because he was eager to learn, he would go out of his way to gain knowledge in any way he could. Few of the other students I taught were as positive as Seth was about his music. Seth lived and breathed music. Music was everything in his life, and that was evident in everything he said or did.

Seth's positivity was contagious. Anyone who met or knew Seth couldn't help but be inspired and motivated. I often found myself so inspired by Seth's positivity after teaching him a music lesson that I would go home later and write a new song or practice my instruments extra hard. Seth's positivity had a lasting effect on me, and I am sure it was the same for many of those who crossed his path. I am grateful to you, Seth, for all you taught me. I will never forget you.

CHAPTER SIXTEEN:

LEAH

(HUMOR)

When I first met six-year-old Leah, she studied Suzuki violin with me and seemed much older than she indeed was. Her maturity, wit, and humor far surpassed her age. Leah seemed more like a twelve-year-old in her intellectual ability and with her use of an extensive vocabulary. I am sure her IQ was at probably above 140. Leah would tell original-sounding jokes, and she made me laugh with her dry sense of humor. I later learned where she got her wit. I met her dad a few months later and, boy, could he tell some whoppers. And when I got to know Leah's father, I felt like I had just met a professional comedian. His jokes were right out of Comedy Central or *Saturday Night Live*. He could have easily auditioned for one of the popular shows and agreed to do stand-up comedy. Leah's mother was just the opposite. She was as serious as they come, and she was a medical doctor working as a general practitioner. That goes to show how opposites can attract. It appeared that Leah preferred the lighter side of life by following in her father's footsteps rather than adopting her mother's approach of being so serious all the time. Let me tell you, Leah's humor worked. She kept me in stitches all the time at each lesson.

It's funny how Leah followed in her father's footsteps except when she mentioned what career she wanted to pursue when she grew up. Leah wanted to be a doctor, like her mother, when she became an adult. But sometimes what we wish to become when we're children doesn't turn out to be what we do when we become adults. Leah became enamored with music, and her passion for the violin and voice grew stronger every year, so strong that Leah decided to major in violin and minor in voice. I helped her audition for a beautiful private music school in South Carolina. She was accepted and offered a full scholarship in the violin, where she played with the university orchestra.

Even though I am sure Leah's mom and dad wanted her to become a medical doctor, they were so supportive of her in her pursuit of a violin performance degree with a minor in voice. They encouraged Leah every step of the way and attended each and every violin lesson until she was too old for her parents to observe her music instruction. Her dad and mom attended every one of her concerts and recitals, unlike some parents who avoided the concerts like they would avoid a contagious disease.

You would think every parent would be supportive of their children, but unfortunately, that wasn't always the case. I found it disappointing that some parents were not very supportive of their children's music instruction. In all the years I have taught, I have also seen parents who were very negative or discouraging. Perhaps they were treated this way by their parents, teachers, or some family member. That is why I found Leah's parents' enthusiastic and robust support of Leah to be refreshing, and it positively inspired me. Whenever I had parents who were sitting on the fence about allowing their child to continue taking music lessons or who wanted their child to quit, I always referred them to Leah's mom and dad. Her parents were glad to talk to any of the doubting or discouraging parents. Leah's parents were like my cheer team as they were highly supportive of me and my teaching.

Leah's parents were so kind to me in every way and showed me the utmost respect. I was always amused and flattered by the formal way Leah's parents addressed me. Even though I made it very clear I was working on my PhD in music education but did have a doctorate, they continued to call me Dr. Cline. I guess they had more faith in me that I would complete my doctorate than I had in myself. They still call me Dr. Cline up to this day even though I never completed my PhD. Maybe they had bestowed an honorary doctorate on me without my knowledge. Perhaps somewhere in a far-off land, there's an honorary doctorate degree waiting for me. Wishful thinking, huh?

Nevertheless, Leah's parents treated me as if I were a part of their own family. They included me in many of their events, such as Leah's confirmation in church, her special school events, and her graduation. I fondly remember being invited to lunches and dinners with her family after Leah's violin lessons. She and her parents would bring me gifts for no reason or bring me some fresh chocolate chip cookies when she came to her music lessons. Leah's parents were always showering me with kind words, praises, and gifts. I felt so much love from the entire family, and I surely felt like I was an important part of Leah's family. When one of my first books was published, *Practice Personalities*, and I toured the area around Atlanta, Georgia, Leah and her parents came to one of my book-launching signings to celebrate with me. At that time, Leah attended a nearby private college in South Carolina and happened to be home for fall break. After the book signing, Leah's parents took me to lunch and treated me like a celebrity. They were so proud of me, and you could tell it was genuine, as if I were one of their own.

The year before Leah graduated, she and her best friend, Landon, decided to record and produce a Christian pop album. Together, Leah and Landon wrote the songs, but they contacted me about the possibility of recording one of my songs, "That Was Yesterday," which Leah had heard a few years earlier and always loved. I permitted Leah to record my song and issued her a mechanical license to do so. She recorded my song with her vocals and Landon's productions. I was honored that a former student of mine recorded a song I wrote. Landon and Leah mixed and mastered their album and sent me their first copy. I was thrilled beyond belief. The album was very professionally recorded with great vocal and production work.

There was more big news that followed. Not only were they graduating, but they were also getting married. Leah and Landon invited me to their graduation and their wedding. Now, that's what I call becoming a part of their family. Today, Leah and Landon have a mission where they tour churches all over the country and perform the songs they wrote, and they often include my song. Leah sings and plays her violin while Landon plays piano and guitar. I have yet to see them perform, but the first chance I get, I will make a determined effort to attend one of their concerts.

I suppose I had some influence on Leah's life by teaching and mentoring her. But Leah was already born with some unusual gifts and talents. She was already going to make her mark in this world. But I am glad I was a part of her life, and God gave me the honor and privilege of being able to teach Leah. Leah taught me how to laugh more and have more fun in life from a serious classical musician's point of view. Her humor and wit rubbed off on me. After a short while of teaching Leah, I began to employ humor with my other students. I still utilize those tools today with all of the students, and let me tell you, having a sense of humor goes a long way toward reaching students. Seeing the lighter side of life makes a very long day seem shorter and makes teaching fun. After the first day I met Leah and her parents, my teaching has changed to the point where I enjoy myself more and have an enjoyable time teaching my students. In general, my life has changed from being an intense, serious classical musician to becoming more of an easy-going, laid-back, and fun person. I am still a responsible and mature adult, but I don't take life as seriously as I used to.

Leah also reminded me about how much steady, consistent hard work pays off. Leah was so self-disciplined in her approach to life, yet so humorous and witty. Leah could suddenly surprise me with a funny and witty joke in the middle of a Mozart violin concerto, or she could suddenly play her violin while placing it on top of head or behind her back. I remember one time Leah showed me how she could play a difficult song on her violin lying on the floor while telling a joke at the same time. I am not sure if Leah was born with humor and wit or whether she learned these traits from her parents. Whatever the case, Leah possessed many admirable qualities and attributes, which influenced me.

I will never forget you, Leah, and you and your parents will always hold a special place in my heart. You will always be family to me, and I am genuinely grateful to you for all you have taught me.

CHAPTER SEVENTEEN:

STUART

(PERSISTENCE)

Stuart was twenty-four years old when we first met. It was the most unusual and unexpected way of meeting a new student. I lived in Nashville, and Stuart resided in New York City, yet we never met in person, and I never taught him in person. I met Stuart in a roundabout way via China. No, I didn't meet Stuart in China, but I was invited to attend an international music conference in Chengdu, China, a few years ago, all expenses paid. I was part of an eleven-member delegation representing Nashville, which included some high-powered CEOs of entertainment companies, Nashville City Council members, Nashville recording artists, and powerhouse music lawyers. During my visit to Chengdu, I met one person I clicked with, Darren from

Vancouver, British Columbia. We hit it off from the moment we met and discussed the possibility of working together on different projects. Darren gave me one of his books on the music business, and I later mailed him one of the music books I had written. We are currently working on a book together about the music business. But meanwhile, Darren has helped me tremendously by sending me aspiring students to coach online about the how-tos of songwriting.

One day out of nowhere, I got this email from Stuart in New York City, asking me to coach him with his songwriting and to help him to become a hit songwriter. I answered it, not knowing who this person was or how he found me. But later I learned that my Vancouver friend, Darren, had referred Stuart.

At first, my schedule was full; I wasn't sure I would have time to teach Stuart. I asked him to wait patiently until I had some openings. A day turned into a few weeks, but Stuart was so passionate that he wouldn't let me forget him. He enthusiastically reminded me he was still alive and that he wanted to learn about hit songwriting from an expert like me. I was finally able to rearrange my schedule so I could make time for Stuart and give him the two hours a week he swore he needed. So, I set Stuart up for songwriting coaching via FaceTime. (I always had to remind myself of the one-hour time difference between his eastern standard time and my central standard time.)

Stuart was so determined and passionate about songwriting that I believe he would have been following up with me and persuading me to teach him even if I didn't have those two-hour slots available to work with him. Stuart's persistence was refreshing and contagious. His positive traits quickly rubbed off on me.

Stuart was so humble and down-to-earth that he never talked about his "real job." But I was curious about Stuart and was anxious to know what he did for a living. He lived in a lovely high-rise apartment in the middle of Manhattan, and he seemed to live a lavish lifestyle. I was curious how a twenty-four-year-old could afford that kind of lifestyle, knowing that his one-bedroom apartment in the middle of Manhattan would easily rent for between $3,900 and $4,500 a month. That means Stuart probably had to make at least $100,000 a year just to maintain his lifestyle. Or Stuart had some very wealthy parents who footed the bill. I realize none of this was my business, but I wondered, nevertheless. So, I googled Stuart to learn more about him, and boy, did I get a surprise!

I learned that Stuart had graduated from Stanford University—one of the most prestigious and expensive colleges in the US—and had received a full scholarship with all expenses paid for his four years at college. Based on the 2020 tuition, and room and board rates, Stanford costs $74,570 a year. So, it would have cost Stuart nearly $300,000 for four years to receive a bachelor's degree if Stuart or his parents paid out of their pockets. That is a hefty amount, but the article I found online revealed that Stuart had received Stanford's full ride on a baseball scholarship. Do you realize how difficult and rare it is to receive a full ride with a baseball scholarship to attend a college as prestigious as Stanford? It is unique and difficult, indeed. The article said that Stuart was hired immediately out of college at age twenty-three to play shortstop for the major league team, the Boston Red Sox. Stuart signed a $10-million-dollar deal.

I realize many professional baseball players earn way more than $10 million, but $10 million still seems like a lot of money for a twenty-four-year-old to make fresh out of college. Immediately after reading that article about Stuart, I suddenly realized I was teaching a celebrity. Although I was excited and honored to be teaching a pro baseball player, I never let Stuart know how I felt about his celebrity status. I was always calm, collected, and professional when I taught him via FaceTime. I was careful to never gawk or act giddy around him.

In one conversation, he mentioned how he had played ball seriously since he was three years old. That was when I asked him what he did for a living and how he was able to support his songwriting habit. We then discussed the realities of the music business. I acted as though I didn't know what he did for a living during our discussion. Stuart mentioned nonchalantly that he played shortstop on some baseball team. It was like no big deal to Stuart, and he treated it like playing ball was just another job anyone could have. That was the only time we ever talked about his work or his baseball career.

Stuart and I spent most of our time concentrating on songwriting. He had a lot of talent and a passion for songwriting. He was interested in writing and producing EDM music (electronic digital music), which is mainly performed at raves, nightclubs, and festivals. DJs create tracks called "mixes" to play in nightclubs for those who want to dance. Stuart was quite a skilled producer of EDM, but he lacked in lyric and melody writing. That was where my teaching and coaching songwriting skills were beneficial to Stuart. I admired Stuart's persistence in reaching excellence with his songs as he would pick and rewrite his melodies and lyrics until he felt they were perfect. He would work on a song until he thought it was ready to record. Stuart's hard work, self-discipline, and persistence were an inspiration to me. I believe he learned his self-discipline and perseverance through all the years he played baseball on different teams from Little League to now the Major League. It is admirable how Stuart was able to continue working as a full-time Major League baseball player while at the same time training as a music producer and songwriter. Stuart was a good manager of time and knew how to be efficient with his schedule. He was an inspiration to me in how to manage my own time in my life.

I am not sure how much influence I had on Stuart and how much he learned from me as his songwriting coach, but I can say that I learned much from Stuart while I was teaching him. My work with Stuart was a reminder that hard work, persistence, and determination are necessary to become a success at anything. Stuart was so particular in perfecting his music that most people wouldn't have the patience to continue with his methodology. Most people would have given up early in the process. I do not doubt that if Stuart continues his super meticulousness and perfectionistic tendencies toward his songwriting, he will become a very successful songwriter. I also admire Stuart's deep passion for his songwriting. He has inspired and influenced me greatly, and I have employed several of his positive traits with my teaching.

I am genuinely grateful that my Vancouver friend, Darren, introduced me to Stuart and for the honor to be able to teach Stuart. I am glad our paths crossed, and I am a richer person in heart and soul for having taught Stuart. Thank you, Stuart, for inspiring me and helping me to add another dimension to my life.

CHAPTER EIGHTEEN:

THE CONCLUSION

They say, "You are what you eat." I have found that to be true my whole life; however, I would take that one step further and say, "You are who you are influenced by." And of course, my wife, family, and friends have made me the person I am today. I would have to argue that my more than six thousand students have also made me the person I am. And while I haven't learned everything there is to know about myself and life (no one ever does), I continue to learn from my wife, family, friends, and current students. Every one of my students has taught me to be who I am today, but some individual students, whom I can't forget, stood out from the crowd.

As I wrote earlier in the book, I remember these students for various reasons, not necessarily because they were all excellent, outstanding students. Each one of their disappointments, failures, victories, and accomplishments taught me many valuable lessons. These lessons were beneficial in making me a complete person. The lessons taught me important and valuable techniques and methods for future use with my students. More importantly, they were also useful in helping me to be a more caring, empathetic, compassionate, and loving teacher for future students and in my life in general. I can honestly say I am a far better teacher and person today than before I met my students.

I would like to think that, in some small way, I contributed to the success and well-being of each one of my students and that I left their lives in a little better shape than they were before I met them. My philosophy in teaching over the years has remained the same, and I always let the students and parents know my philosophy on the first lesson when we first meet. I tell them that my goal is to teach the love of music first. While some of my students will become music professionals, my goal is *not* to teach my students to become professional musicians. I tell them stories (including my own story) of what a rough life it is to live as a professional musician. I describe how many musicians have to struggle to make ends meet. Sure, some very successful musicians have gone on to become famous and earn more money than they could ever spend in their lifetimes. But they are few and far between, and I don't ever want to subject my students to that kind of life. If they become professionals, that is good. If they become enormously successful as musicians, that is great. I never go out of my way to discourage any of my students from becoming professional musicians, unlike so many music teachers who tell their students to quit or tell them they could never make it in the music business. Who am I to tell someone that discouraging news?

There are so many stories of music teachers telling their students to quit because they don't have what it takes to make it, and then years later, those students become super successful in music. Those students got the last laugh. Regardless of whether my students become professional musicians, it is essential to note that I have trained many students to become great connoisseurs and consumers of music. They are some of the audiences who attend the symphony, ballet, and opera today. They are some of the consumers who purchase classical albums and classical iTunes selections now. Many of my students use music as therapy, relaxation, and a hobby when they come home from a hard day of working on a job that has nothing to do with music. And some of my students perform in amateur, adult community orchestras, where they receive no compensation except for the joy they get from playing the instrument they love.

Out of the numerous qualities and traits my students have taught me, the most predominant quality is patience, followed by empathy, compassion, persistence, and hard work. Other characteristics I have learned from students are joy, love, hope, passion, drive, encouragement, determination, ambition, humor, creativity, wit, courage, and positivity. And while I will probably learn many more lessons from my present and future students, I am grateful for all the lessons I have learned from my past students and what they have helped me to become today as a person and a teacher. If I had the chance to live my life all over again, I wouldn't change anything. All of my students came into my life for various reasons; some I know about, and others I am still trying to figure out. I believe I was supposed to meet every one of my students and to teach them in the way I did. Teaching isn't necessarily about what the teacher can teach the student, but it is also about what the teacher can learn from the student. Here's to all the students I'll never forget. Thank you.

QUESTIONS TO THINK ABOUT

Are you a teacher or a former teacher? If so, what important lessons have you learned from your students?

Are you a student? If so, what important life lessons have you learned from your teacher?

Who was the most challenging student you ever taught? What made that student challenging? And what did you learn from that student?

Who was the most challenging teacher you ever had? What made that teacher challenging? What did you learn from that teacher?

Have any of your students helped you to become a better teacher? If so, how?

Over the years, who were students who stood out as memorable and whom you will never forget in your lifetime? Why did they stand out above the rest?

Do you believe students come into teachers' lives for specific reasons? Do you believe teachers come into students' lives for specific reasons? If so, what are some of the reasons?

What are the best and most inspiring moments that have ever happened to you as a teacher? Why do you consider them to the best and most inspiring?

What are the best and most inspiring moments that have happened to you as a student? Why do you consider them to the best and most inspiring?

If you had to do it all over again, would you still teach? If yes, why? If no, why?

Do you ever hear from any of your past students? Have any of them ever praised you for what they learned in the classroom from you? How does this make you feel? How does it change you?

Have you ever reached out to any of your past students to let them know what you learned from them? If so, what did you tell them?

These questions are to provoke your thoughts and for your personal use only. But if you feel led to share some of your stories, please send them to me at ThorntonClineauthor@gmail.com. Who knows? I might even ask for your permission to publish them in a future book of the *Who's Teaching Who* series.

ACKNOWLEDGEMENTS

My special gratitude goes out to God, Paul Shepherd, Roberta Cline, and all of the students and parents for making this book possible.

ABOUT THE AUTHOR

Ever since his mother signed him up for piano lessons at age five, Thornton Cline has been writing nonstop. With over one thousand published songs and 150 recorded songs, Thornton Cline has been nominated multiple times for Grammy and Dove Awards. Cline has been honored with "Songwriter of the Year" twice in a row by the Tennessee Songwriters Association International and received a platinum certification for sales of over one million album units in Europe. His songs have been recorded by Engelbert Humperdinck, Gloria Gaynor, Rebecca Holden, Gary Puckett, Tim Murphy, Ray Peterson, Billy and Sarah Gaines, Tammy Trent, and Matt Newton, among others. Thornton Cline has had his original songs appear on TV and in major films. Cline has had seven of his songs reach number one, and five songs reach the top 10 on the Billboard charts, Euro Indie Network Top 100 charts, World Indie Top 100 charts and the official US Top 20 Countdown. Cline was recently inducted into the

Songwriters Hall of Fame by the Tennessee Songwriters Association International in Nashville.

Cline has also written twenty-six adult and children's traditionally published books, and he won the first place Maxy Literary Award in 2017 for "Best Children's Young Adult Book." Several of Cline's books have reached the top 10 Amazon charts.

Cline is an in-demand author, musician, songwriter, and speaker. He lives in Hendersonville, Tennessee, with his wife, Audrey, and their cat, Kiki.

Made in the USA
Middletown, DE
24 September 2022